Broken Promises
One Family's Journey Through Alcoholism to Reconciliation

By
Jane Bartels

with
Tansy Howard Blumer

For my children, Kris, Hallie, Lindsey, Courtney and Tyler, who came back into my life with grace and understanding.

Amazing grace! How sweet the sound
That saved a wretch like me!
I once was lost, but now am found;
Was blind, but now I see.

— Christian hymn; words written by English poet and clergyman John Newton; published in 1779.

Contents

Author's Note

This is the true story of my life as I remember it. However, I have altered the names of some of the persons in the book to preserve their privacy.

Preface

For thirty years I was a slave to twin addictions and could not find the person I was born to be.

By some miracle, after years of desperate scrambling, falling back repeatedly and then scrambling some more, I was finally able to climb out of the pit I had fallen into; but not without inflicting major damage on a lot of people. Somehow I eventually got past the addiction to alcohol that was killing me. Only then was I able to make something of my life. I am fortunate that I still had time to change who I had become and begin to lead a useful life.

Something mysterious and unexplainable happened to me at a very low point in my life. It gave me strength and enabled me to overcome my addiction to alcohol. And eventually, I no longer had to struggle with bulimia, my secret alternate addiction.

After thirty years of addiction, I am not sure I will ever truly like or even respect myself again. But I am trying to get past this with the help of my children who have sufficient reason *not* to want to help me at all. I am grateful that I now have clients who trust me and let me work with them to help them shed their own addictions.

If you read my story and see some of yourself in it, please keep in mind the following list. It is my list of the things an addiction does to a person—things that made me a stranger to myself for many years. You will recognize *all* of these things in my story. I was the most addicted person I have ever known.

I want my list to energize and motivate the people who read it, help them recognize the problems similar to their own or a loved one's, and make them sincerely want to find a way out of the pit.

Addiction does these things to you:

1. It breaks up your family;
2. It diminishes your self esteem;
3. It makes you do crazy things;
4. It creates in you great shame that is almost impossible to erase;
5. It makes you become a different person—a person you don't like;
6. It makes you completely self-centered;
7. It isolates you from other people and causes you to withdraw from society;
8. It makes you afraid to try to change;
9. It diminishes your spirit and dulls your spirituality.

I have written this book to tell the truth about myself and to make amends to my family and others for all the hurt that I have inflicted on them. The things I did while under the grip of a powerful addiction created a ripple effect that harmed my family in more ways than I can bear to count. The voices of my adult children throughout the book have helped keep me honest in the telling of my story and demonstrate the painful range of destruction and misery that one person's addiction brings to a family.

Kris's Preface

As Jane's oldest child, I feel that I am in charge of keeping this story honest. First I should say that it is not just Jane's story. There are two stories here; hers and the story of the five children she left in order to drink. You will hear from all of us as Jane's saga progresses. But you will hear from me the most throughout her story, because someone needs to point out what was happening to us while our mother was cycling in and out of rehab and detox and living apart from us--often as an unemployed and hopeless drunk—while we children were just trying to grow up.

In her preface, Jane tells what addiction does to a person. In my preface, I list the things that addiction does to the children who love an addicted person. You see, addiction seldom damages only one per-son— the addict. It has many victims. Jane's children all survived our harrowing childhood, and now we are all prospering despite the damage done to us. Many children of addicts end up living the very same life as the person who made them miserable. We were lucky because we avoided that.

Being the child of an addicted person does this to you:

1. *It destroys your faith in who you thought your parent was;*
2. *It makes you wonder who will protect and love you;*
3. *It makes you resentful;*
4. *It robs you of your childhood and forces you to grow up too quickly;*
5. *It causes you so much pain that you have to take antacids while still only a teenager;*
6. *It forces you to cry silently because you don't want to show your true feelings;*
7. *It scars your heart;*
8. *It shows you how strong the love between siblings can be;*

9. *It makes you stronger; you just won't realize this until later in life;*
10. *It makes you try to become the kind of parent you fantasized about;*
11. *It makes you thankful for a loyal step-parent;*
12. *It makes you sad about the years that have been lost;*
13. *It turns you into someone you don't recognize at times;*
14. *It makes it hard to smile when life as you know it seems so serious;*
15. *It forces you to put on a brave face when people ask how you are doing.*

It takes time, but as you heal, it becomes very clear that life is short and forgiveness is not only possible, but is necessary for your own soul. Because I love my mom, I decided that if she could kick such a horrible addiction, I could forgive her and move towards building something new by including her in my life!

BROKEN PROMISES

CHAPTER ONE

Awakenings

Oh shit, back in detox again, I thought as my eyes opened slowly and quickly slammed shut against the familiar artificial light of a hospital room. Even in my numbed and confused awakening, I am aware that this is a worse-than-usual detox for me and that I have come closer to the edge of extinction than ever before. This time I am lying in a bed in a private room, not yucking it up as I have often done with the familiar detoxing drunks from the Farmington, Connecticut streets and rail yards. Generally, I am welcome at the center of any ragtag group gathered together in broken fellowship in an emergency room to be monitored *en masse*. At those times, we good-time buddies avoid looking at the painful truth of our lives while clutching cups of cold decaffeinated hospital coffee and aiming our still half-drunk pleasantries towards the nurses. Those seasoned pros have heard and seen it all, yet they still try hard to smile tolerantly at our antics while checking our vital signs and monitoring our fluid intake. Sometimes their facial expressions reveal something different; an automatic disgust for our failure to outrun our demons. These looks are becoming quite familiar to me.

This time, I am staring through an alcohol-tinged fog at my cool, detached insurance company executive father who sits stiffly across the room on a molded plastic hospital chair with his herringbone tweed overcoat folded neatly in his lap and absent-mindedly still wearing his dark brown fedora. If he has said anything to me yet, I am not aware of it. This is an unaccustomed occasion for both of us. Usually, I am on my own in detox, having been dropped off at the facility by addicted friends and lovers who make their excuses and quickly turn away at the door in order to avoid entering the uncomfortable smells and activities of the place. As far as I know, my father has never set foot in a hospital to observe me in this state—although there have been numerous chances. I find myself wondering idly if he is the one who brought me here, but do not ask.

He is watching me guardedly, and I see in his expression something I have never seen before. I imagine—more clearly than my sodden state might normally allow—that this is true sadness I am seeing; a deep, dark, despairing sadness. His mood surprises me and makes me wonder if my face has been smashed in or if my scalp is hanging from a flap of skin. For it seems to me that only such visual horrors inflicted on a daughter's pretty face would cause that expression on such a buttoned-up father's face.

That fleeting expression of emotion disappears as my father suddenly stands, lifts his hand in a half salute, and disappears down the hall on his way home to join in our family's traditional Christmas Eve. From down the hall, I can hear nurses and staff calling out cheerful Christmas wishes to one another, and soon after, my father's low voice exchanging polite holiday greetings with a pleasant-sounding woman.

Alone again, I gaze idly at the jungle poster on the wall. It has started to shimmer and the creatures and green jungle underbrush have started to come alive. The scene grows larger and brighter by the minute, and all the animals are on the move—their procession suddenly and silently filling one wall and spreading to the next. This lively scene is more than enough to distract me, and the memory of my father's visit is soon lost in the haze of such an entertaining hallucination.

It was probably on that very night that Millard Bartels—Bart to his friends—went home and wrote this obituary to announce the death of his only daughter:

Jane B. Ronald, daughter of Millard Bartels of West Hartford, died at her home in Farmington on ___. She was 43.

Born in Hartford she lived most of her life in the Greater Hartford area. She graduated from its Junior School, Oxford and Bennett College of Millbrook NY, and attended Smith College in Northampton, Massachusetts. She had been a member of the Junior League of Hartford and did charitable work in this community.

In addition to her father, she leaves two brothers, Thomas of West Hartford and Bruce of East Bloomfield, NY, and five children, Kristine Stewart of West Germany, Hallie Stewart, a student at Roanoke College, VA; and Lindsey, Courtney and Tyler Ronald of West Hartford.

A memorial service will be held in St. John's Church. Burial will be in the Fairview Cemetery of West Hartford at the convenience of the family. Memorial contributions may be made to Kingswood-Oxford School in West Hartford.

Twenty-three years after that night of jungle DTs, and long after my father's death, it is my two brothers who bring out his handwritten draft of my obituary—a prototype of WASP restraint—and show it to me. Tom says, "Dad thought you were going to die that night and told us it just seemed sensible to have an obit ready."

Not knowing of its existence until that moment, I am stunned and mystified by it. What kind of father coolly writes the death notice of a living, breathing daughter? Was this just Millard's peculiar way of coming to grips with my terrifying addiction? Was his pen assigning me prematurely to the grave in a last attempt to manage what was already completely beyond his control? Or was it his orderly lawyerlike way of tying up loose ends after witnessing for himself the inevitability of my early death? Why did he lie and say I died at home? And why didn't he mention my dead mother, Eulalia Stevens Bartels? As a proud and devoted fixture of Hartford society, she surely would have expected to see her name in *The Hartford Courant*, no matter how sad or horrifying the occasion.

When my father's own drunken father, Herman—after ruining Bartels Brewery, the second generation family business in Syracuse, NY, and running through all the remaining family money—abandoned his wife, young son, and a daughter in order to spend the rest of his life drinking himself into oblivion, his son must have made a solemn personal vow to never again speak of or to this embarrassment of a father. Years later, when he received a phone call from the Salvation Army of Chicago informing him of his father's lonely street death from alcoholism and asking him what to do with the body, he answered coldly, "That's your goddamn problem!" And then he slammed down the phone and went off to bed where he presumably enjoyed a full night's sleep uninterrupted by any ghosts of the departed. Perhaps his decision to write my obituary was a variation on a familiar Bartels theme—disposing of that which makes you uncomfortable. Only this time, it is a cherished only daughter—unmistakably cursed and besotted with her grandfather's alcoholic genes—who he banishes to the grave with carefully calibrated, socially acceptable newspaper wording.

CHAPTER TWO

ꕥ

The Birth of Loneliness

"No wonder you drink." Those words must have come as music to my ears. Otherwise, why else would I remember them so clearly 34 years later?

For the first time in my life, I was seeing a psychiatrist and was confident that he was going to figure out what was so wrong with me that I—the alcoholic mother of five beautiful children—had recently submitted voluntarily to the abortion of a sixth child because he and I both doubted that I could care for it properly. After he met and talked with my psychology-averse mother, that four-word summary served as his not-very-professional opinion of what was wrong with me. His words gave me what I fervently sought; a pat reason for my messed-up vodka-soaked life. In my mind, I was off the hook now. I could simply blame Eulalia, the cold, socially ambitious mother who continued to rule my life with an iron fist well into my adulthood. She was the mother I wasn't strong enough to get away from and my tolerant second husband's worst nightmare. *She* was the reason for my drinking!

Armed with what I eagerly accepted as a reprieve absolving me of personal responsibility, I opened up to Dr. Howard, regaling him with all the sad childhood details that came to mind. I spun my needy and delusional web around him, selectively giving him all the information about my life that would lead him to further clear me of any responsibility for my condition.

Now that I am a successful professional therapist, I see and freely admit that for many years I warmly embraced the role of victim because it was a convenient way to avoid examining and confronting my own behavior and the addiction that was at its core. But that is *now*, and my story begins with *then*. Then is when I began regaling Dr. Howard with the story of what I told him was the first and perhaps the greatest crime my mother committed against me...

When I was eight, my mother—anxious to live in the style to which she had been accustomed while growing up as the much younger daughter in a wealthy industrialist's family—moved our family from a comfortable corner of West Hartford, Connecticut to a house which my friends called "the mansion on the hill."

My first neighborhood had been filled with young families whose lawns were crisscrossed with the well-worn paths we children made between houses and across adjoining backyards and empty lots where we played endlessly. During the daytime hours we stayed outside, thoroughly engrossed in neighborhood-wide games of Capture the Flag, rolling trash cans down the hills in boisterous contests, waiting greedily for the Good Humor man to arrive in the afternoons, and going inside to watch *Howdy Doody or The Lone Ranger* on TV only when it was raining or too dark to play outside.

In those carefree days, I was an active daredevil of a girl who loved playing rambunctious games and joyously participated in my brother Bruce's mischievous adventures. Like most of the children of that time and place, the wonderful benign neglect underlying the parenting practices of our parents allowed us to independently explore the woods, try out risky tricks on backyard play sets, and visit other children's houses without prior arrangement or parental supervision. Parents were alien creatures anchored in a parallel universe, thankfully oblivious to our enthusiasms and pastimes, and apparently unconcerned with the kinds of unseen dangers which cause today's parents to hover and fret over the smallest details of their children's lives. In those days, families regularly came together for meals, but as soon as the words, *you may be excused* were spoken, we children eagerly escaped the polite restraint of dinner table rituals and played throughout the neighborhood until darkness and bedtimes drove us indoors.

Technically not a mansion, our new address was nevertheless an extremely large new house—cold and sterile, spotless and technologically up-to-date—located close to the exclusive Hartford Golf Club and much too far from that well-worn and lively neighborhood I loved. Along with our move, my upwardly mobile parents' brand of benign neglect began to feel like something closer to abandonment. The attention I began to get from them had to do mostly with the laying down of boundaries between me and any other children, and my mother's intense efforts to make me wear clothing and hairstyles I despised.

Some of my friends were riding horses regularly, but my father apparently thought I was too fragile or too incompetent to be around them and forbade it. In such matters, he acted as if I were a delicate and priceless porcelain doll in which he had a substantial financial investment rather than a genuine fatherly interest. When he did show interest in me, it was usually only as a belonging to be admired by and embarrassingly dandled on the knees of his visiting male colleagues. As their conversations turned away from me and back to talk about work, hunting, or golf, he had a way of dismissing me in a certain hurtful way; with a wave of his hand pointing to the other end of the house. There I returned to my solitary amusements, more confused and alone than before.

In those early years, sadness and aloneness kept me from seeking out close friends after school. Old photos show me with a forced happy smile, but when the 'say cheese' part did not happen, the sadness of that little girl just oozes from the picture. But depression was never spoken of in our family in relation to any of us. If my parents used that word about someone they knew, their disgust was intense and uncompromising. Giving in to such weakness was unseemly—something that happened to others, but not to members of the Bartels family.

I often lay beneath a big old maple tree in our yard and stared at the sky. I imagined animal shapes in the passing clouds and wished I had wings so I could fly away from that lonely place called home. I was a caged bird and often wondered where I would go if I could fly free. But then I worried; *If I fly away, how can I take care of myself? Who will help me, listen to me?* These moments of hopelessness and self doubt only deepened the ever-present sadness, and hot tears often burned my cheeks.

I spent much of my time upstairs alone in my pink and green bedroom accented throughout with chintz ruffles and flowered wallpaper. My mother had chosen this girly décor more as a dream of what her only daughter should want than any acknowledgement of my actual preferences. Her frequent room inspections made me afraid to make a mess and careful not to leave anything out of place. To protect against the crushing silence, I kept the little white radio at my bedside turned on all the time. Strains of newly emerging rock 'n roll music thrilled me and—when I was sick or on vacation—an avid love of soap operas like *Stella Dallas* and *The Guiding Light* helped me stave off the solitude and fill the growing void.

As I grew older, my mother began to indoctrinate me with her puzzling attitudes about female aspirations. "Girls don't go to good colleges, boys do," she often intoned, as if it were the word of the gospel. To this pronouncement, she always added, "To do well, girls need to marry the right man." And then she added the subversive advice meant to turn me into her version of a Stepford wife; "It is not your role to stand up to men; it is your role to please them." That must have been how she saw her own role. But as far as I could tell, she never succeeded in pleasing my father in any ways that I could observe.

In the early days of life in our large, soulless house, one side of my bedroom was neatly arranged with the army trucks and cowboy and Indian accoutrements I had saved from my brothers' toy collections, and in another part of the room my Storybook Dolls stood lifelessly in orderly rows. I came to think of those dolls as "the happy family"—a beady-eyed, compliant group for whom I imagined an extraordinarily happy, perfect and loving family life quite unlike my own. I played with them for hours, but when I craved more physical action, I piled up sofa cushions in the basement play area, turned a dog leash into a set of sturdy reins and rode my imaginary pony for hours to the recorded strains of Gene Autry's soothing voice crooning, *Back in the saddle again, out where a friend is a friend...* I had begun to inhabit the persona of a lone cowgirl on the Western plains surveying a broad landscape devoid of *kemo sabes*.

When I think of those endless hours, I grieve for the little defenseless girl I was, and view that type of lonely play as an embryonic form of the detachment which is still a troubling component of my psychological profile. Too many times, I drifted up alone from the basement where my imaginary horse was stabled, climbed up the massive circular staircase in my silent house, and threw myself down on my bed, crying for no specific reason. Those hot tears rolled across my cheek time and time again, and I idly tasted them with my tongue while listening passively to the sobs coming from within me. Such sessions were inevitably ended by the sweet sound of our maid Rosie calling me for dinner.

I was a princess on a pedestal—loved, I suppose, but inexplicably left there forgotten or ignored until the next adult viewing was to occur. I began to feel that any slip-up on my part could mean the end of my father's already scant regard for me, and I developed an anxious fear that one wrong step would turn him against me forever. After his death in 1997, I found a letter which I had written to him from camp. The words—carefully drawn on a sheet of birch bark—read: "Dear Daddy, I will be better when I get home. I love you with all my heart, Janie."

Recognizing the desperation of this anxious birch bark pledge today, I realize that I wasn't writing about any particular personal misdeed. Instead, it seems that I was trying to insulate myself from his actual or future disappointment in me by making an all-purpose pledge to become a better person. But I was already a good child—shy and obedient—and I had no idea what I might have done to warrant his indifference. As I saw it, sending me to a camp I hated was his idea of punishment for things about me that displeased him.

Or perhaps that sad pledge etched in birch bark had more to do with my secret guilt and confusion about something that had occurred earlier that summer. My oldest brother Tom—nine years older than I—had come home from his freshman year in college and while presumably as bored, lonely and confused as I was, invited me into his bedroom and engaged me in a rudimentary sexual give-and-take that stunned and confused me. Looking back on this disturbing tableau, I can only think that he was as lonely and desperate for love as I was, and that using me in this way was something he had not consciously intended or even understood. While this incident disturbed and repelled me, I came to believe it might be what true closeness meant.

Whatever the reason for my brother's actions, that strange incident further nudged me to the edge of a stubborn, numbing depression that stayed with me in some form or another for many years. I have come to believe that this event in my young life might have jumpstarted my eventual belief that my sexuality was the one and only thing I had going for me; the only thing I had that could draw people close to me. Whether or not this was the igniting incident, the fact is that for many years I operated on the belief that my sexuality gave me power and was my only personal attribute throughout the numerous affairs I entered and then routinely destroyed during my addicted life.

Born of two German immigrant parents, my father seemed almost a caricature of all the usual German stereotypes; unbending, undemonstrative, unforgiving, and coldly detached. I have only scant memories from childhood of father-daughter activities with him. These included the few instances in which he played chess with me and when, noticing my natural athletic ability, he hit tennis balls with me to help me master the game. Only one rogue memory stands out in which it seemed that the two us of briefly shared a vision. We were walking in a field side-by-side when I suddenly blurted out, "Daddy, wouldn't it be wonderful if we could buy a farm and have animals and live there forever?"

"Yes," he agreed, looking down at me with his face softening a bit. Then he hesitated long enough to make me believe in my childish innocence that he was seriously considering the idea. But he replied with what seemed to be regret, "Your mother would never consider moving to a farm. Don't waste your time thinking about it."

There was plenty of evidence that my mother would never have appreciated the earthiness and simple pleasures of life on a farm. She wanted to control nature, not submit to its charms! She herself was the embodiment of control; a carefully-crafted Madame Tussaud's wax figure with her unmoving hair always in a state of permanent-waved perfection. I never saw her wearing a pair of slacks and can only guess that she deemed them inappropriate to her social status. Her everyday clothes were perfectly tailored and from only the best designers—with an emphasis on Chanel—and she took pains to wear jewelry that was substantial and authentic. Even her forearms were subjected to her ruthless search for perfection as she regularly shaved off the peach fuzz that dared to grow there. Although I did not witness her most private personal ablutions, she submitted me to regular enemas to 'cleanse' my young innards, a long-standing requirement that years later resulted in surgery to remove several feet of my intestine that had been damaged long ago by the practice. If this was her idea of how to keep a child's digestive system clean, I can't imagine what ridiculous and unwise procedures she might have inflicted on her own interior.

To expand their social world, my parents entertained 'the right people' regularly at our house. My brother Bruce, always engaging in daring antics, drew me into his favorite subversive party game—planting plastic dog feces and stunningly realistic vomit among the expensive cashmere overcoats of the gentlemen and the mink tippets of the ladies which were piled high on a guest room bed during parties. We also planted whoopee cushions in sofas in the living room where guests chattered noisily while drinking and smoking prodigiously. These petty crimes created a feeling of closeness between my brother and me and kept the coldness of our household briefly at bay.

Bruce's brand of naughtiness was especially courageous and bold given that he and Tom were well aware of the physical side of our father's displeasure. The boys were terrified of his dark references to what he called, 'the reminder in the closet,' a stick he used on them when he considered their behavior sufficiently out of line. This was one aspect of home life in which my lonely position on the family pedestal was a desirable thing. As the only girl, I was spared any form of physical punishment. But Bruce developed a significant stutter which might have been a reaction to the 'reminder in the closet' and all it implied. Tom simply grew more outwardly compliant while oddly detached. There was another victim too. When my father was displeased by the activities of my beloved Weimaraner, Baron, he showed no hesitation about beating him in front of me with a different reminder—a leather dog's leash—or picking him up by the scruff of the neck and shaking him angrily.

Baron was a gentle soul and my constant companion in those days. He routinely waited for me to come home from school, watched me endlessly as I played with the 'happy family' or rode my sofa cushion horse. A tolerant dog, he even allowed me to dab Chanel #5 behind his ears to 'freshen him up.' But one day when I returned home from school, Baron did not come running to greet me and his sudden disappearance from my life was never discussed or explained.

I had been lonely before, but with Baron gone and Bruce sent to boarding school to be "shaped up" as my father described it, I felt more desperately alone than ever.

Rosie, our cook, provided a measure of the warmth and emotional support I craved in those days. I sensed that she cared about me and welcomed my presence in the kitchen despite the fact that my mother required her to wear a maid's uniform and answer a bell when her services were needed in the dining room.

Rosie was an ample Cherokee Indian/African American woman who fed me comfort food, baked treats for me, got me through puberty, and shared with me her lighthearted philosophy of life and love. She had false teeth but rarely wore them, causing an endearing lisp. I loved hearing her soft and sooth-ing tones. When she heard my mother disparaging me about my incompetence, she would later hug me privately and croon softly, "Gurl, you are so pretty, you can do anything you set your mind to." To this day, when I see a woman of Rosie's general physical description, I always feel a warm, comfortable surge of affection.

Rosie lived in the servants' quarters over the kitchen and was occasionally joined by her alcoholic husband Osgood when he was between jail terms. Osgood was a good-hearted man and added to the fun and warmth in the kitchen during his brief times in residence. He provided some emotional support to the lost child I was, but it was Rosie who was my ever-present per-sonal social worker and cheerleader.

I was popular at school but rarely invited friends over to visit. I knew they were intimidated by my mother's presence and by the lack of warmth in our house. In those days, my mother picked me up at school in her big showy Cadillac, and when she arrived, I always jumped in quickly and ducked down in the soft leather backseat to avoid the stares of my schoolmates whose mothers drove more reasonable cars. She never asked about my day and I assumed it was because whatever I had done, it wouldn't be what she would have wanted. I envied my friends because their moms seemed so happy to see them after school.

At our house, Rosie was always busy cleaning or cooking, but she still found the time to listen to me, help solve my problems, and laugh at my antics. Unfortunately, she was illiterate and thus could not help me with the homework that was a continual source of frustration and failure for me. It seemed to me that my parents were resigned to the fact they had a stupid kid and thus never even tried to help me with my homework. And so I struggled alone and routinely took shockingly error-filled work to school the next day.

I still remember with a shudder those arithmetic problems which filled me with confusion and my inability to memorize even one simple line of poetry. There just seems to be a part of my brain that does not work. I assume it is the pinball machine part where my concentration bounces around like a lead ball pinging on various targets and bouncing off randomly.

After wrestling alone with homework, I often lay on my bed fighting back the tears and waiting for my mother to knock on the door and offer these last orders of the day; "Jane, put on your PJ's right now and go to sleep." Neither parent ever came in to say good night or talk about my day. When it was time to turn off the lights, I generally closed my eyes, pretended I had wings, and cried myself to sleep.

Kris

Why is it so hard for me to picture my grandmother the way my mom does? I assumed all women of that generation were formal, dressed-up, and stiff. Nevertheless, my grandmother and I had a lot of fun together and I loved the inflexible daily structure in her household and the smell of clean laundry in her house. Yes, Grandma was big into manners and being polite, but I also felt she had a warm quality. Mom was scarred from the way her mother treated her and the loneliness she felt in that house, but I felt safe there. Obviously, she was very lonely and depressed over what she felt was a lack of love and attention in her household. But I thought of Grandma's house as a refuge from the growing chaos of Mom's household as her drinking got worse.

The incident Mom told about her brother is very difficult to comprehend because he is my uncle and I love him and find it hard to believe this happened. I didn't want to believe the story at first—because of her drinking, Mom's truthfulness was always in doubt— but her story of the events so many years ago has never wavered. If you knew my uncle you would be shocked because he is the kindest, most loving uncle ever. He was someone I could always trust to watch out for me while I was growing up. Both my uncles treated me like I was their own child and I will forever love both of them. Crazy, isn't it, that I can love someone despite hearing how he caused emotional pain to my mom when she was at a very vulnerable stage?

Mom didn't have it easy and her experience of being in that house and my experience were different. Grandma and Bawpa (what we called our grandfather) made me feel special when I was there. Maybe they were making up for all of the mistakes they made with Mom and her brothers. Their house certainly was a lonely house on the hill and I felt it took on a more sinister tone when the lights were off at the end of the evening and the burglar alarm was set for the night. The deep silence—with the exception of the regular chiming of the grandfather clock— kept me in my bed praying I wouldn't have to get up and go to the bathroom in the middle of the night. Oh, it was so quiet… Maybe that sinister silence is what my mom remembers. As much as I loved being there, my imagination went wild: Was the alarm really set?

Could a burglar be detected? Would the alarm go off if I got out of bed? I decided I would play dead if an intruder got into the house. I even practiced playing dead.

Unlike Mom, I always enjoyed sleeping at my grandparents' big house. Yes, the house was stiff—everything bleached, ironed, clocks chiming followed by silence—and I often wondered if it had been this quiet for Mom. There certainly were times when I would fall asleep thinking how lonely it must have been growing up in that house with everything in order, her bedroom set apart from the rest, the smell of roses and soaps permeating her bedroom. I would pour through pictures of my mom when she was young and spend hours studying the photo albums Grandma kept of all of us kids. My grandma ran the show and it was tough for me to tell if she was even happy. But I always felt that she loved all of us kids and my memories of her are still close to my heart. Overall, Mom and Grandma appeared fine together on the surface. But Grandma would have covered things up if they weren't great. It's what she did.

Did mom go to sleep as a child feeling the same way I did? Maybe she practiced her dead person imitation too. Maybe my wild imagination came from her. Once the sun was up, I always felt much better; free to roam around the house safely. I often went into Grandma's room and talked about trivial things while she was getting ready for the day. I loved to go through her jewelry and try everything on. Most of her jewels were purchased during her travels with my grandfather. She had a beautiful aquamarine set and told me that one day the set would be mine because it reminded her of the color of my eyes. I will always remember fondly her saying this to me. Today, I have that beautiful set and cherish it with all my heart. Why couldn't Mom go into Grandma's room and talk about things the way I could? It seems so odd that she and I have such totally different childhood memories of the same person.

Both Hallie and I got to stay with Grandma's warm and gentle sister Maymi. I was under the impression, based on Grandma and Maymi's households, that everyone had a maid dressed in crisp white uniform who could bake like nobody's business. Like Grandma, Maymi also had a sterile house with fresh pressed linens on every bed and a chiming grandfather clock. Meals were formal at Maymi's, but the atmosphere was a little more relaxed than at Grandma's house. I don't know why, but Mom was taken to Maymi's house to heal once when she ran into a wall while chasing Hallie and busted her nose. I always wondered how she managed to run into a wall like that. I felt guilty about her getting hurt but thought; *How could she not see something right in front of her and then barrel into it? Was she drunk when it happened?* Mom was destined to break that nose more than once because of her drinking. It's amazing to me that she still has a perfect nose.

Mom thought she was raising us differently, but really, my childhood wasn't too far off from hers. When I was ten or eleven, we had our own version of her big lonely house on the hill after we moved from a small, cozy house in a kid-filled neighborhood—where I always felt secure—to a huge house on a hill in a different part of town. Mom assigned me to a big cold room on the third floor, but unlike her mother she allowed me to choose my own decor. I chose lime green shag carpeting and lemon yellow plaid wallpaper for that room and it made things brighter. But I was afraid of that part of the house and considered it haunted. As I lay there, sleepless, I worried that there was a ghostly mother on the fourth floor who seemed to be rocking her child in a chair while the child bounced a ball endlessly against the wall.

Imagine this: one night shortly after we moved into our own big house on the hill, I was sitting at a desk doing homework with only a single desk light shining on my paper in the darkened room. Suddenly I was startled by an unfamiliar voice nearly shouting a loud "Hello!" A young woman was standing in the shadows staring at me! I was afraid to move, thinking she might be there to hurt me. But she must have sensed my fear eventually and explained that her name was Betsy and she lived down the alley in a neighboring house.

I blamed this intrusion on Mom's sloppiness and inattention. I thought; Not only have I been moved to a freakishly big house on the hill, but strangers can walk in whenever they want! Betsy's parents came to retrieve her and explained that she was mentally challenged. I grew to like Betsy when later I saw her around the neighborhood, and eventually I stopped having nightmares about strangers entering my room to stare at me, or worse.

I wonder, was my experience of being lonely and isolated any different than Mom's? I wasn't allowed to say anything about the move or the choice of where my room would be because it didn't matter that I was scared; this was where Mom wanted to live and that was that. No one ever bothered to go up to the third floor to see how I was doing. Mom was busy with my younger siblings and as I look back, I think she just kind of forgot about me.

I will always remember with a shudder a night when I heard the sirens of a fire truck responding to a house fire across the street. Alone in my faraway room on the third floor, I became terrified that the fire was at our house and everyone had fled, forgetting to alert me. I remember smelling the horrible stench of the fire as I rushed down the stairs and outside to see what was happening. As I stood in the street facing the burning house, I watched as the paramedic brought out a stretcher with a body on it covered in a sheet. The gruesome sight of that gurney gave me nightmares for a long time afterwards. As I watched, I saw a woman's heavy leg slip off the gurney to reveal a partially melted stocking stuck to it and a pink slipper dangling from the lifeless foot. The paramedic saw my panicked face and quickly pulled the leg back and tucked it under the sheet over the rest of the body.

We kids didn't know this woman or what her life had been like, but I wondered if she drank just like my mom and thought of a phrase I had often heard: You never know what goes on behind closed doors. No one outside our family really knew my mom; people only knew what she wanted them to know. But those of us inside the house knew better; we saw the dark side. I worried that the burned and dead woman on the gurney could have been my mom. I guess I never stopped worrying about things like that.

As my mom grew sicker with her drinking, my grandparents' house became a safe haven for us, and I was thrilled when I could sleep there instead of on the third floor of my own house. I was comfortable at Grandma's, and just smelling the clean, ironed sheets on the bed made me fall asleep instantly. I was thankful to have my sister Hallie stay with me at Grandma's because I wanted to protect her and make sure she was okay too.

Like Mom, I was shipped off to camp when I was still in elementary school—I guess this was to build character and make me independent. Or maybe it was a way for her to have one less kid to take care of. Mom wasn't there to get me settled at camp and she wasn't there to pick me up or send me a care package. It was my grandmother who picked me up in her giant Cadillac— like the one that embarrassed Mom. She and Maymi came together; dressed up and acting like the Baldwin sisters, those two rich elderly spinsters in *The Waltons* TV series. I remember how they stood and patiently watched me while I completed my final riding task before we left for home. Unlike Mom, I was allowed to ride horses, but I had to borrow boots from my counselor because no one at home read the list of things to pack for camp. After that summer, I was required to go to camp every July. Mom thought she was raising us differently and not in her mother's autocratic style, but the similarities were there nevertheless.

We didn't have a Rosie who wore a white dress and clean white shoes and whose presence created a warm feeling in us. Instead, Mom hired a series of bizarre cleaning ladies who seemed to me to be possessed. She must have been drinking then because her hiring practices were pretty sloppy. One of her hires came to work wearing her wig backwards. Another one often pooped in the backyard and then stored the feces—wrapped in paper—in the closets. Still another helper gave me a mood ring and said she could 'control me' with it. That started my fearful imagination running overtime. Where did Mom come up with these terrifying people?

I knew in those days there was something not right with my mom but I was still too young to know what the problem was. One day I came home from a skateboarding accident in tears and held up an injured wrist. "You'll be fine," Mom snapped while continuing to prepare dinner. When my stepfather—Pop—came in from work, I showed him the injury and he asked Mom why she hadn't done something about it. "I thought she was exaggerating," Mom answered. As it turned out, the bone was broken.

Mom complains about her mother's emotional neglect and her envy of other kids whose mothers picked them up at school with such happiness. I wonder if her feelings of motherly 'neglect' were similar to those my sister Hallie describes:

Hallie: I used to fantasize that Mommy would be there after a cold soccer practice and have the heat blasting in the car like the other mothers who waited for their kids. But I had to ride my bike home shivering with the cold because she didn't come. When I had my children, I became that mother for them—the mother who is always there and always has the heat on in the car. Several therapists have told me that because of my experience growing up, they are shocked that I am the kind of mother I am. I have always been nurturing and loving with animals and children. I make their little lunches, and cut their sandwiches in neat sections.

As her drinking problem progressed, Mom's shortness and snappiness in the early evening was becoming a regular occurrence in our lives. Looking back, I see that Mom was desperate to drink and possibly was overwhelmed by having so many children to care for. It often seemed to us that we were in her way. Eventually, I figured out that she was trying to get dinner together quickly so we would settle down for the evening and she could sneak away from us to get her drinks. We hated seeing her be so cranky and her sharp tone of voice cut us like a knife. Now, when I read her story, I begin to see how desperate she was for alcohol; so desperate, in fact, that she was beginning to put her kids on the back burner.

CHAPTER THREE

ᕬ

The Person Everyone Wants to Be

My maternal grandfather, Chester Stevens, owned a thriving paper business which included four operating mills. He was a classic American-style self-made man who lived in a massive, cold Tudor house and was chauffeured to work daily in a limousine. I remember him as a stern old guy who looked like Winston Churchill, chewed continuously on a fat cigar, and frequently used a golden spittoon when he felt the need to spit inside the house—which was often.

As I grew older, I noticed a streak of anger and resentment that seemed to fill my mother when we were in the Stevens house for the mandatory stiff, formal Sunday dinners we often attended. It was no secret that Chester, who already had a beloved first-born daughter, wanted his second child to be a son who would eventually take over the business. His disappointment with my mother's gender must have been obvious to her, and I often wondered if that could be the source of the jealous rages she aimed at her gentle older sister Maymi throughout the years. Whatever the cause, I developed a cautious sense that my mother's rage against her sister could easily turn on me and I learned to avoid doing or saying anything that could set her against me and cause her to use that unbearably shrill and infuriated voice. Her anger, simmering just beneath the surface, became for me the dreaded equivalent of the 'reminder in the closet' with which my father kept my brothers in line.

I also became alienated and afraid when my mother's many prejudices exploded into words. It seemed to me that she singled out entire countries, religions and races for her sweeping hatred. Africa was a dirty word. Irish Catholics were the lowest form of life. Without provocation, she often said menacingly to me even before I began dating, "You will *never* go out with an Irish Catholic as long as I am in charge!" Jews were also the target of her unrelenting superiority. Since she and I seemed so very unlike in temperament and general mindset, I often wondered if I had been adopted and worried that she didn't like me because of whatever country I had come from or the religion of my real parents! These free-ranging worries and her frequent outbursts drove me further and further into my own world.

Unlike those ladies of Hartford who never spoke of or showed off the old money wealth which had been passed down to them through several blue-blooded generations of their families, my mother chose to let her family's 'new money' define her. She was so obvious in her pursuit of social prominence that she was depicted by name in Stephen Birmingham's book, *The Right People*, as a social climber. Although she was willingly interviewed for the book, she was so humiliated by the author's ironic comments about her in print that she compelled my father to put on his lawyer's hat and go to the local library where he got the first edition of the book banned from its premises. Having accomplished that, he demanded and got a retraction from the author.

Given my shoddy academic performance in grade school, there were plenty of warning signs that I had substantial learning difficulties. Nevertheless, my upwardly mobile mother made sure that I was accepted for the seventh grade at Oxford, an exclusive and competitive private girls' school with a tiny enrollment. Here I was to struggle with poor concentration and sub-par learning skills until I barely managed to graduate. Thankfully, I was never reprimanded or singled out by my teachers for poor performance, but they didn't give me any special tutoring or remedial work either and I struggled mightily.

When I was fourteen, I took a summer babysitting job with a family in Hyannis Port, Massachusetts. It was only a two-week job, but I hated babysitting and didn't have anything to do when I was off-duty. In an unhappy frame of mind one day, I started idly sampling the baby food puddings I was supposed to feed to the baby. Almost immediately, what had started as innocent 'sampling' became a strange compulsion to eat as much of it as I could get my hands on. I managed to gobble down an astonishing amount of that pudding in two weeks. Always a trim girl, I nevertheless put on just enough weight to feel bloated and overweight for the first time in my life.

When I got home, I said to my mother, "I feel so fat! I'm going on a diet." She responded by raising her voice to that terrifying screech, "You will eat whatever is put in front of you! That's the way it is!" In my usual passive manner, I simply stopped talking and obeyed her command. But I thought while eating the compulsory meals; *If I make myself throw up, Mom won't be mad at me and I'll be able to lose this weight.* Thus I eagerly adopted a strangely satisfying habit of bingeing and purging.

I had never heard of a psychologically-based problem called bulimia—nobody I knew had ever mentioned that word or the concept. But I was to learn later that it was the official name for the nasty little secret I acquired that summer. Bulimia is widely recognized now; the data shows that it can be triggered by a reaction to a careless phrase or incident. Also, about 90% of all eating disorders start because of some form of sexual abuse. So it was that both triggers were present in my case; unknowingly, I was a poster child for bulimia!

Whatever the origins of my eating disorder, it seems to have been a complicated outgrowth of a messed-up psyche and it stuck with me even longer than the addiction to alcohol which ruined my life for thirty years. Together, the two addictions were to take over my body and soul—a dynamic duo of addictions which gave me a way to comfort myself, release the unbearable stress I felt, and escape temporarily from a growing number of psychological demons.

My mother had always made it clear that Oxford was the 'right' place for me. But it was during my high school years that my escalating eating disorder and my embarrassment about my woefully inadequate academic skills placed me outside the norm. I began to hide food in my bedroom. Gobbling down entire boxes of donuts, various kinds of cereal, and stale loaves of bread followed by purging gave me an emotional escape from the loneliness and confusion that was always throbbing inside me.

When I was in tenth grade, my mother saw evidence of my purging on several occasions and took me to our family doctor for an examination. During the visit, she sat woodenly in a chair, leather purse in her lap, listening while I continued to cover up my deepest secret. The doctor asked, "Jane, are you throwing up because you feel sick or because you are upset?" Hedging my bets because Eulalia was staring at me, I replied, "Well, I have thrown up a couple of times, but not for any special reason. I just felt kind of sick I guess."

What else could I have said with my mother sitting there in judgment? After our brief and unrewarding dialogue, the doctor turned to her and said, "Well, Mrs. Bartels, Jane is a very healthy girl physically. But if this problem continues and we can't find something physically wrong with her, I might decide to send her to the Psych Department at the Institute of Living for observation."

That scared me. I can only speculate about how Eulalia was reacting because she revealed nothing. I assume she was thinking there was no way she would allow a member of our family to end up in a psych ward. After we left the office, she never again spoke of the problem or engaged me in any kind of discussion about what was going on with me—ever. Like all the most distasteful things in our family, she simply pushed this strange little aberration under the rug.

But the doctor's comments had put me on alert and made me more secretive about hiding and consuming my edible contraband and the compulsion began to gain strength. For me, eating all this food had little to do with actual hunger or a love of food. It had evolved as a way of coping with my deepest, saddest feelings. My secret relationship with food was providing me with a private world—a place where I had total control over my own actions, where I could call my own shots! Eulalia was never welcome in this strange dark place.

Even when I was in high school, my mother still unfailingly laid out my wardrobe each day. On one particular morning, I briefly found the courage to challenge her iron control by saying, "No way am I going to wear that stupid skirt." She stared at me with a look of extreme shock which then morphed into one of burning hatred. Then, after a heavily-laden pause, she tore into my closet, throwing all my clothes onto the floor and screaming, "You ungrateful brat! Maybe you don't need any clothes at all! Maybe you can just find some rags to wear out on the street! Maybe you don't even want to live here!" The way she looked at me and the sound of her high-pitched screaming as she threw the clothes around have never left me. That morning I became permanently terrified of her.

Somehow the escalation of my mother's rage translated to an overwhelming feeling in me of shame which evolved into an oddly recurring feeling which I came to think of as a state of 'frozen tears.' The walls were beginning to build inside me and my fear of losing my identity was now mixed with these new feelings of shame. I began having dreams about falling from clouds. During those dream-filled nights, I awoke often with a painful knot in my stomach—a feeling like that caused by speeding on a roller coaster ride, terrified of falling, but with no way of stopping the ride or the fall.

Any ability to stand up for myself was long gone, lost somewhere in that big, sterile house. The obedient but carefree tomboy of my early years had become a sad, people-pleasing teenager. As I came closer to my high school graduation, the photos of me began to show a puffy face caused by the bulimia and a fixed, fake smile—like that of a threatened and frightened wild primate. Even the slightest confrontation brought up huge waves of physical anxiety within me. The resulting need to purge allowed me to relieve my pent-up frustrations and simmering anger towards all the adults around me.

My academic life continued to be a struggle; all my friends were slated for Seven Sisters colleges like Smith, Vassar or Wellesley while I was headed for a junior college. There, according to my mother, I could pass two years comfortably while shopping for a husband with an Ivy League degree who would be from what she called a 'good family.'

Despite my academic deficiencies and my low self esteem, I had a dedicated and enthusiastic group of school friends. Many years after graduation and after my drinking problem had become well known, a group of us gathered at a class reunion and someone exclaimed, "Jane, you were the person everyone wanted to be! We thought you were perfect!" I was truly shocked, especially when others chimed in: "You were so lively and pretty!" "You were such a wonderful athlete!" "You had so many boys in love with you!" And, "We loved that you were always willing to share boys with us and help us get dates!" Ginny Means, a best friend from childhood who went to Smith College and later practiced family law in New York City, said, "I always wished that one or two of your boyfriends would begin to notice me." Then she laughed, adding, "Some of them did pay attention to me, but they did so mainly to ask me what they could do to get your attention." As things often go in life, it was Ginny who ultimately found the perfect man and has been successfully married for many happy years while I struggled through three difficult marriages and a long string of unsuccessful relationships, only finding peace and happiness with a fourth husband when I was already a grandmother.

My family was Episcopalian in the WASP style—that is, with restraint—and I was not a particularly religious girl. Nevertheless, in high school I was inspired by William Sloane Coffin, the chaplain of Yale University, when he came to speak at a religious conference I was attending with some of my school friends. Coffin was just becoming famous as a leader of what evolved into the civil rights and peace movements of the 1960s and '70s. When I heard him speak, I became interested in the possibility that there could be a spiritual presence in my life with the power to take me out of my own self-centered concerns. I felt changed by Coffin's words and ideas in ways that I could not articulate at the time. But the elemental feeling of spirituality which arose in me at that time was to reappear dramatically later in my life when I reached the lowest points of addiction and despair.

Betsy Morgan, my best friend in high school, was a very smart girl who was always placed in the most skilled academic classes. But despite the enormous academic gap between us, she valued our friendship as much as I did. I loved going to her house where her mother served us fresh-baked treats from her oven and music filled the air. Understandably, Betsy was intimidated by the formality of my parents when she came to my house. During meals she nervously watched me to find out which of the many implements at her place setting she should use. To make things worse for her, she felt strongly that my mother did not like her. She was right; Eulalia thought Betsy was less attractive than she wanted my friends to be, and although Betsy's father was an Ivy League graduate and had once worked for my father at the insurance company, my mother said to me, "He and his family are simply not in our class." She then added, "*And,* he's a drunk!" making it clear that she thought Betsy's family was disgraced by the taint of alcohol abuse. In view of the Bartels curse of alcoholism, her failure to acknowledge the irony in that remark is laughable.

Betsy was not the only accomplished young person to fail Eulalia's standard for social acceptability. My brother Bruce was invited to attend a prom at a private girls' school by a girl he liked and with whom he had a nice friendship. When my mother learned he had accepted the invitation, she secretly called the girl and explained coldly that Bruce was "unable" to take her to the dance after all. When Bruce found out about this, he was humiliated and deeply hurt. When he angrily confronted her, our mother enumerated her reasons as if they had a shred of legitimacy: "Her family is Jewish and her father is only the general manager of a clothing store. Barbara is simply not in our social class, so just forget about the friendship, Bruce. It won't work."

My mother was always thrilled that I had lots of male suitors. At the same time, she did not want me to do anything that would damage our social status in Hartford. When as a high school junior

I went to a college weekend at Williams College and willingly—even enthusiastically—had intercourse with a wonderful, bright frat boy, I earned Eulalia's fearsome wrath. My memory of this is fuzzy, but since our maid Rosie's sex education tips had not included anything useful about birth control, I believe I panicked after the loss of my virginity and told my mother that I might be pregnant. On the other hand, I was experimenting at that time with ways to rebel passively against her iron rule and I might have offered her that information in order to get the inevitable dramatic response. If so, I was not disappointed.

I was not pregnant, but my announcement brought out my mother's executive tendencies. She duly summoned the boy and his very prominent parents to a meeting at our house. The details of the meeting are not entirely clear after all these years, but I do remember that his family was at the very top of the Hartford blueblood social pecking order, a fact which greatly mollified Eulalia. Basically, the two of us got off with a stern warning, and during my last year of high school, she monitored my social activities a bit more closely.

It was during this period that my father chose to break the news to Eulalia that he had a mistress—a bright, accomplished woman who practiced law in Washington, DC—and he would like to be freed from his unhappy marriage in order to be with this woman. My mother had always been intimidated by career women and had made a habit of declaring that they were all lesbians. I had often heard her disparaging them for the tailored professional clothes they wore and mocking their high intelligence and achievements.

Confronted with the news that her husband was not only having an affair, but—even more appalling—that the woman was a lawyer, my mother became unglued. She started to drink heavily and within a short time became a consistently irritable and short-tempered shrew. There were even several notable occasions when she stepped over the boundary into crazy-land and drove around Hartford at night wearing only her nightgown while crying hysterically and weaving all over the road.

During the day, she was depressed and listless, and her friends became genuinely concerned about her. There was even whispered talk about her possible need for psychiatric care. But my father's response to such suggestions was to state unequivocally, "No one in this family needs psychiatric care in any form." My mother took some of her despair out on me by increasing her control over my wardrobe and hair and ending the only activity we had ever enjoyed doing together—our occasional girls-only trips to Broadway to see theater productions.

My parents were now drinking and arguing all the time. After two drinks Eulalia always managed to turn to the subject of my father's affair and she never lost an opportunity to use her bitter sarcasm against him. Her repeated allusions to his misdeeds were now added to the cutting repartee she had used for years to ridicule his mother and sister for being financially needy and for dressing and grooming unfashionably as if, as she put it, "just off the boat from Germany."

My confusion and anxiety levels rose to the max when I overheard or witnessed her vicious attacks, but it seemed there was no one to go to for guidance. My brother Bruce—possibly the only one who could have protected me from the damage this unhappy union was causing on a daily basis—was long gone from the household. It was only many years after my parents' deaths that I learned he had a good idea of what life was like at home after Eulalia learned about the affair. In one of my last phone conversations with him before his own death, Bruce said, "Jane, I feel a lot of guilt about my inability to protect you, my little sister. You needed to be shielded from our mother and from life in that big lonely house."

Predictably, Eulalia was adamant in her refusal to go along with a divorce. Anyone who knew her at all knew that further discussion was futile. My father ultimately gave in to her browbeating and emotional blackmail and agreed to stay in the marriage, undoubtedly choosing to continue his affair *sub rosa*. Whatever the bargain was that my parents struck, their marriage clearly had taken a dark and precipitous downward turn.

After the battle lines were drawn, a resentful Bart began to feel justified in making obvious passes at the most attractive and social of their Hartford acquaintances. Stories of his horny antics on social occasions still circulated in Hartford for years after his death. For her part, my mother turned her attentions more and more to her volunteer activities, spending less time at home than she had before the trouble began. When they were together, the two seemed to agree that drinking was a good way to anesthetize themselves.

Although I had not been one to experiment with liquor or any other forbidden substances, I was fully aware of the reliance on alcohol as a social and psychological lubricant in my family, and began to think that it might work for me. One evening, late in my junior year of high school, I used alcohol for the first time to help me feel more relaxed and seductive while entertaining a new boy in my life. Whoever he was—presumably a student from nearby Trinity College —I knew that my evening with him would probably turn into a make-out session on the basement couch, and I felt anxious and awkward about that. Thus, in a state of mild discomfort, I went into my father's den and opened the liquor cabinet, pouring myself a shot of his favorite Bourbon and swallowing it in a single gulp. As the elixir slid down my throat, it warmed my entire body and made me feel whole and connected. I stood there transfixed, enjoying the instantaneous sense of well-being and warmth and realizing that it was the best sensation I had ever experienced. In seconds, I was changed from an anxious little teenager to a confident—even seductive—woman. The tingling I felt was the first blush of what would become my love for alcohol and the promise of what it could do for me in any number of other situations.

Oddly, the warm sensation summoned by that first taste of alcohol was associated in my mind with the vivid feeling of happiness I had achieved at a younger age while playing with my imaginary family or opening my first present on Christmas morning—that singular, magical time of the year when our family seemed connected with one another. How pathetic it seems now that when I later crossed into the darkest stages of alcoholism, Christmas became the saddest time of year for me due to my self-inflicted disconnect from family and friends.

Professionals who deal with addiction refer to this initial profound reaction to alcohol as a "set point" in the brain which lingers over time and enables a person to connect repeatedly to the memory of an experience when something made them feel especially good. For a person like me who is already predisposed to addiction, that memory can be an accident waiting to happen. Although I did not turn into an alcoholic overnight, it would be only a few more years until my addiction to alcohol—at its core a genetic gift directly from Grandfather Bartels—began in earnest. Given all the hundreds of gallons of alcohol I consumed over the next three decades, it is that life-changing first reaction to it that I remember more vividly than almost any other sensation of my life.

Kris

Mom's memories of her parents' drinking, their cocktail parties and her first taste of alcohol in their house remind me of some of my memories of the role alcohol played in our house. When I was quite young, I was oblivious to what an alcoholic was or that my mother was drinking around the clock, and I assumed it was normal to have so much alcohol around the house. But I always noticed how loud people were when they drank and how loud and crazy my parents' parties became! It is amusing to remember that the fridge in the basement wasn't grounded and it shocked anyone who opened it to get more alcohol. There were plenty of people being shocked by it because there were always cases of beer in that fridge and plenty of thirsty drinkers. As I got older, Pop often counseled me that beer and wine were safe, but hard alcohol was dangerous. At other times he told me that when I was old enough to drink, I should always drink hard alcohol straight, because "those candy drinks will make you do stupid things!"

Mom's vodka bottles were everywhere in the house, put just out of our sight. Eventually she was trying to hide them from Pop's sight too. I remember after finding one of her bottles with a little remaining vodka in it, I decided to pour some laundry bleach into the bottle to see if she would notice. I waited for her to try to sneak the vodka like she always did by mixing it with one of her diet sodas. I secretly hoped she would swallow some of the bleach. I imagined that would make her realize magically that I was onto her and then she would stop drinking as a result. But nothing happened. Maybe she was so wasted that she drank the bleach and didn't know it was in there; I will never know.

As I got smarter about Mom's alcoholic ways, I often asked if I could have a small sip of her soda, claiming that I was thirsty. Boy, did that get her going! I knew I could get a reaction because she had something to hide from me! I didn't challenge my mom much, but I could see that this drinking thing was not good for her or for us. There were times when she took my younger siblings to the store and then forgot where she had parked the car. She repeated this pattern often enough that I hoped it was a problem with her brain and was not caused by drunkenness. But eventually I knew I was kidding myself; so much for trying to give her the benefit of the doubt.

As Mom's drinking began to catch up with her, I was quick to get the kids out of her sight to avoid hearing that sharp tone she used with us. We all loved our mom dearly but as I got older, feelings of resentment started to brew. Her illness was forcing me into a much more serious role which I had no choice but to accept. I adored my siblings, so babysitting and helping out more at home really wasn't hard for me. I watched them walk and talk for the first time and loved to snuggle with them and tuck them in at night. Being a mother seemed like such a natural role to me. The unfortunate part was that I wasn't even in high school yet.

Mom got worse, and then the arguments between Pop and her grew too. I watched Mom pull away from my stepfather when he showed affection. I sensed she wasn't happy and thought she didn't seem to love him. As anyone who knows him will attest, Pop isn't the easiest person in the world, but he has a heart of gold and would give you the shirt off his back if you needed it. I felt sad for him. He sent Mom into rehab programs but nothing was sticking. My mom just wanted to drink—I guess she wanted to erase whatever it was that was ailing her.

Mom's parents were trapped in an unhappy marriage when she was a kid. But our mom left us when we were just kids! When she did, it was in the summer before I began high school. The shock and sadness as Pop and I tried to keep the troops together is permanently etched in my brain. My little brother was still in diapers! Who leaves their young kids like that? Obviously, a very sick woman does.

My high school years were tough because I felt so much responsibility at home. I had sports to keep me busy after school but nothing erased the constant sadness I felt deep in my heart. I couldn't be light-hearted around my friends. I couldn't relax my body enough to act my age. I knew Pop was doing his best but I also knew that he needed me to help out at home. I felt I had to be there to support him. My English teacher, Mr. Poirot, pulled me aside one day to tell me to "stop and smell the roses." He said it broke his heart to see that I rarely smiled and said he didn't want me to miss out on one of the best times of my life. His heart was in the right place and I will always remember what he tried to do for me. But no one could pull me out of my funk.

I had a wonderful group of girlfriends and while they tried their best to pull me up and get me to have some fun, I just couldn't respond. I badly wanted to be like them. I wanted to have a mom at home who was interested in my day. I wanted to talk with her about the boys I was interested in, and I wanted to feel safe and cared for. Since I couldn't have any of that for myself, I did my best to show my younger siblings how much I loved them. I wanted them to feel safe. They had Pop, but a mother's role is special. I wanted to fill Mom's shoes and do a much better job for them than she was doing with me.

Unlike Mom's first drink—a tip-off to the power alcohol would have over her—my very first drink was in 8th grade at a classmate's Bat Mitzvah. I was new to the school and wanted to fit in, so when some kids sneaked sweet and sours from the bar, I joined in. I don't know how many I had, but I do know that when I arrived home my father was entertaining friends. By then, I couldn't stand up straight. Both my father and friends laughed about this as if seeing a drunken 8th grader was quite normal!

Fast forward to my junior year in high school; I didn't like drinking but it was the end of the year and I thought I should try to loosen up. After too many drinks, I really 'loosened up' all over the grass outside a classmate's house. This time I had followed my stepfather's advice to drink alcohol straight rather than in mixed drinks. Did I feel good or relaxed after that? NO! I hated the taste of alcohol; it burned my throat and made me feel weird. My unfortunate date had to carry me to my friend's car and my friends wrapped me in paper towels (in case I threw up again) and put me to bed. The next day felt like I had just died and something had rotted in my mouth!

My bad hangover along with the intense heat presented a huge problem because I had to sing with the choir at graduation and attend the junior prom that night. I made it through only one song before the heat took over and I threw up again. My poor prom date—so sorry, Scott—I couldn't have been a bigger drag if I had tried! So much for drinking in high school.

Fast forward to college; I still didn't like the taste of alcohol but found it easier to loosen up if I was drinking. I was far away from all of my family's problems and I felt I had a license to try to be young and carefree. But I was still wound up very tight. When drinking, I would *think, Drink a little more, maybe that will help you escape. But any escape was so temporary and the pain of the following day so awful that I could never imagine how my mother could be doing this all the time.*

Mom's drinking affected all of us in a number of ways—and we all still live with the fallout from her drinking. My youngest sibling, Tyler—the only boy in our family—was so traumatized by Mom's alcoholism that he apparently believed that it was a life sentence for him:

Tyler: I became very familiar with the term alcoholic at a very young age and have always been haunted by it. My lifelong concern has always been; *Am I going to be one?*

BROKEN PROMISES

CHAPTER FOUR

The Invitations Have Been Printed

My visits to the psychiatrist continued. Wrapped in self-pity, I recounted to Dr. Howard the second biggest crime I believed my mother had committed against me—forcing me into a bad marriage...

Eulalia was adept at getting compliance from me and did so regularly. A mean look, a raised voice, even a well-placed sigh from her always brought me right back into line, no matter how strongly I might have felt about whatever the issue was. Simply being in the room with her or hearing her voice on the phone caused a tight knot in my stomach to throb and seize urgently. These became the triggers for my bulimic episodes—my sad way of comforting myself and chasing away that agonizing feeling in my stomach.

According to my mother's wishes, I did go to a junior college. Admittedly, this was probably the only option for me, but I passively accepted that option because she had always made it clear she considered me dumb and incapable of doing better. But I think a stronger motivation was that she believed that the rich girls and New York debutantes who attended that school were the most desirable social peers for me. In any case, while I was a student at this college/debutante mecca I developed a new little secret which surprisingly brought with it some unanticipated good. I was using "diet" drugs dispensed in large quantities by a sleazy local doctor to keep my weight under control. To my surprise and delight, these pills helped me focus on my academic work for the first time in my life. They had the effect of quieting the pinball part of my brain and allowing me to study well enough to pass my exams. Thus I emerged from junior college without a great deal of difficulty and an earned associate's degree in Early Childhood Education.

Eulalia knew nothing of the bulimia or the diet drugs, but she had no trouble learning that I had a boyfriend who was a Princeton graduate. Not one to take things at face value, she secretly hired a private investigator to thoroughly research Adam's family background. After receiving the investigator's positive report, Eulalia gave our engagement her enthusiastic blessing and began arranging a wedding extravaganza designed to bring West Hartford society to its knees. Ultimately these efforts were to be amply rewarded when the actual event was featured on Sunday's then-exclusive wedding page of the *New York Times*.

But I had developed cold feet about my impending marriage almost as soon as we set the date, and not only because of Eulalia's embarrassing excesses. I felt an avalanche of regret when many of my hot college boy admirers called to invite me to various football weekends and I had to turn them all down. Now my commitment to Adam began to look like the end of my youth and all its bright possibilities. After all, I was only nineteen. When I reluctantly declined their invitations, I explained that I was engaged, and the reply was always approximately the same: "Why would *you* want to be engaged?" I knew it was a very good question and had absolutely no truthful answer for it other than, "It's what my mother expects." The mere thought of marriage began to trigger that dreaded stomach knot and the bulimia which I had always associated with my mother. I knew I wasn't in love with Adam and never had been.

In a panic, I began casting about desperately for something that would take me far away from home and give me a reason for breaking the engagement. I decided that the perfect solution was to go to England and become a VSO—the British equivalent of a Peace Corps worker. To his credit, Adam sensed my discomfort and readily admitted that we were much too young to be married.

Relieved, we agreed to break the engagement without blame or unpleasantness.

Thus united in our decision to save ourselves from a terrible mistake, we determined that Adam would be the one to approach Eulalia and tell her the news. Yes, I was too afraid of her to help him! But standing up for the right thing turned out to be a losing struggle for Adam. He quickly backed off in the face of Eulalia's inevitable white-hot rage. True, the wedding was only a month away, but her arguments—that the invitations had been printed and the venues of church and country club firmly booked and staffed—were a cliché and a cop out of the worst sort. She flew into one of her rages and shouted, "I don't want to hear any of your cowardly reasons for backing out of this marriage!" As far as she was concerned, our marriage was a business deal; the ink on the contract was dry, the signatures affixed.

Adam's hasty retreat from Eulalia's angry presence left me the option of standing up to my mother on my own. I had never had the courage to confront her, so why would I be able to now? I believed that I was the last person on earth who could have persuaded her to cancel an event which meant far more to her than to me! Believing that we were out of options, Adam and I were thus frozen in a state of terrified passivity and allowed ourselves to be put through the endless preparations for the society wedding from hell.

Whatever fragile self esteem I had previously managed to gather around my young shoulders now began falling away in tatters, leaving me utterly exposed to the chill of Eulalia's toxic psychological powers. Satisfied that she had won a major battle, she then prepared me for marriage with the best confidential mother/daughter advice she could muster; "Just bite the bed sheet and pretend you like the sex."

Within three months after my marriage, I became pregnant with Kris. I was a baby having a baby! Initially, the notion of having a child meant to me simply that I would now have something to fill my idle days with. And, having offended Eulalia with the near-cancellation of the wedding of her dreams, I felt pathetically relieved to be doing something that was sure to please her. Within a short time, I found that I loved being pregnant, and for the first time in my life, I experienced contentment and a deep sense of purpose. So much so that I didn't always notice how alone—and lonely— I felt in our tiny apartment in a rapidly decaying neighborhood in South Orange, New Jersey. It was here that I was to wile away the days with frequent trips to the local market followed by gorging on the sugar-laden, caloric food I brought home. I spent the afternoons watching an endless string of TV soap operas and purging numerous times before Adam arrived home at night looking just like my father in his brown fedora and tweed overcoat—a look that gave me the creeps.

Directly across the hall from our apartment, a neighborhood pimp regularly dropped in on his girlfriend, and the sounds of their sordid fighting filled the corridor and passed easily through the thin walls of our apartment. I became accustomed to hearing the police arriving on the scene to break things up. For me—a person who had always been sheltered from the seamier side of life—the physical violence and visits by the cops were quite exciting and gave me stories to entertain Adam with when he came home each day from the job he already hated. He ate the appalling meals I threw together while I told him of the day's drama; I admit to a clear memory of serving culinary disasters like tomato soup with greasy cooked hamburger meat floating in it.

Because I was living in New Jersey, it was harder for Eulalia to exercise her accustomed control over my activities. But on one unforgettable occasion, she arrived by car in the afternoon while I was home alone, and almost immediately became incensed about the imperfect housekeeping of our bathroom. She burst out of that tiny room like a shot, shouting at me, "You are a terrible housekeeper! This place is filthy and disgusting!" She then delivered the worst insult she could think of; "You are turning out to be a bad wife!" Following that accusation, I mentally improvised, *and soon to be a bad mother*, as the likely next words from her mouth. She then stomped out of our tiny apartment and drove back to West Hartford, leaving me bewildered and miserable, the rock-hard knot in my stomach tightening painfully.

My mother then began an aggressive campaign to get Adam to change jobs and move back to West Hartford where she could "help with the new baby" and, presumably, manage our household herself. She and my father had plenty of contacts in the architectural firms in Hartford with which to help Adam get connected, and he was eager for their help. Once again, Adam deferred to her power, and we moved into a West Hartford apartment which we found ourselves but which Eulalia insisted on inspecting before we committed to it. Adam was later to remark that this move to West Hartford was the worst mistake of his life. Not counting the mistake of going through with the marriage to begin with, I am inclined to agree.

Our baby, Kris, was about 2 years old when I persuaded Adam to move to a more rural town outside Hartford in an attempt to appease a growing inner restlessness. We found a pretty yellow, cheerful home on an acre of land which got high marks from Eulalia. Kris was a beautiful, joyful little girl; I remember how she used to run to the fence that stood between us and the farm next door to feed grass to the curious cows which placidly accepted and chewed her offerings. And I watched her with a warm and happy feeling inside me. This was the closest I could come to the living-in-the-country-with-animals fantasy I had tried to sell to my father when I was a child.

I began some rudimentary attempts to prepare myself for a meaningful career by taking some courses in Psychology and Juvenile Delinquency at the University of Hartford. But Adam and I had begun drinking socially and our regular attendance at cocktail parties started to dull the edges of my ambition. Alcohol was a magical social lubricant for me and after a few shots, I always became the life of anyone's party. Equally important was that alcohol made me more willing to tolerate my husband who I had begun to actively dislike.

I was a happy drunk, but Adam had an anger management issue when he was drinking and became abusive in certain situations. He shoved me around angrily a few times, and in one particularly explosive incident, he tried to push me out of a moving car. I have no memory of the provocations I might have been guilty of—surely he sensed my growing revulsion towards him—but I was certain that his anger-filled and drunken default mode was a troubling omen.

Almost as soon as we had settled into our idyllic country house, I began to grow restless again. This time I argued to Adam that I wanted to feel less isolated from friends and family and move back to West Hartford. To this day, I cannot understand or explain why I felt the need to get physically closer to my mother, the very person who had made me so miserable for most of my life. Moth to the flame, I guess. Or maybe I had become numb while living beyond my mother's reach and instinctively wanted to get closer in order to be recharged by her raw electric power.

Whatever my reasons, after moving again, living briefly and unhappily in a fixer-upper which we never got around to fixing, we quickly bought a different house, one that seemed just right for our little family. We moved in with my parents for several weeks while waiting to close the deal and it was then that I learned I was pregnant again—this time, with Hallie. Thankfully, although my dependence on alcohol had grown a great deal, I was able to stop drinking entirely without regret and without temptation while carrying Hallie. I loved my babies, nursed them after their birth, and took great pride in being a mom. The pregnancies and the months after the birth of a new baby were the times when I came closest to feeling happiness and fulfillment and I was always open to the notion of having more of them.

Unlike me, Adam did not stop his drinking during my pregnancies, and while arguing with me one day while I was carrying Hallie, he hit me hard enough to cause early contractions which necessitated a trip to the hospital. Our marriage was already in deep trouble and Adam knew it. He had begun staying longer at work and drinking with his friends to avoid being with me. In one particularly sordid tableau while we were living at my parents' house, he and my father got into an alcohol-fueled altercation which ended when my father wrestled him to the basement floor and pinned him until he gave up and sullenly stalked out of the room.

In those days, there was always a cloud of depression hanging over me as my increased reliance on alcohol took the place of developing healthy relationships, particularly with women. This was unfortunate, because I had always been popular with women and new female acquaintances continually tried to befriend me. Nevertheless, I didn't encourage their friendship, and at parties I ignored them and laughed and flirted with the men while I was getting wasted.

Even while engaging in outward flirting and lively drunken conversations, I saw myself as a puppet whose movements had to be supplied by a person working the strings and giving me a voice. Feeling that I had no real voice or viewpoint of my own, I felt dumb in social situations, and when I was not yet drunk, I believed that any thoughts and ideas I did have were certainly not worth sharing.

I was becoming more and more restless, always trying to find some joy in life apart from the simple joys and duties of motherhood. Looking back, I think the constant moving to different houses was an attempt to satisfy the need to constantly change the circumstances of my daily life in order to find some peace. I was still bulimic, but beyond that, I was becoming more and more involved with alcohol, my new all-purpose best friend and comforter. Not satisfied with regular social drinking in the evenings, I was now taking reinforcing straight shots when I was alone during the day. And when I was going through the bedtime rituals with Kris and Hallie, I was increasingly aware of being snappy and short when they begged for another story or another hug. The contagion had begun in earnest; my two innocent and sweet little girls with their normal emotional needs were getting in the way of my own desperate need to begin my evening drinking rituals, and I was often irritated and impatient with them.

When I began to feel alarm about my escalating reliance on alcohol, I checked out several books on alcoholism from the local library and hid them in a brown paper bag to bring them home. The irony of the situation was not lost on me; although I believed these books might help me climb out of the addiction that was beginning to engulf me, I nevertheless felt the need to hide them in a brown paper bag like a drunk hiding an open bottle of booze.

Adam's violent rage at me while I was pregnant with Hallie precipitated the unsurprising end of our marriage. Even if there had been no violence present to justify a divorce, I would have found it easier to simply erase him from my life than to try to summon the patience and skills to work things out and fix our problems. I didn't grieve in the least for our dying marriage. Instead, I began to fantasize about leading a fun, single life, and plunged into magical thinking; living without Adam was going to make me happy! Clearly, the alcohol was already stunting my emotional development and I was regressing.

Eulalia repeatedly tried to talk me out of leaving Adam and warned, "No man will ever be interested in a single mother with two little girls!" But I went to court in Litchfield, Connecticut to testify about Adam's violent behavior, and was granted a swift and efficient divorce. I marked the end of our marriage by immediately flying to the Caribbean with a friend.

Adam did not feel the relief that I did with our divorce decree in hand. In fact, he was so devastated that he arrived at my Caribbean getaway begging me to reconsider so we could try to work things out. In my mind, I was *free at last*, and no degree of persuasion and promises by Adam could convince me to take him back. My drinking, no longer characterized by regret over my unhappy youth or unwanted marriage, now became openly celebratory.

I was gleefully on my own now—a divorcee with a two-year-old, a four-year-old and a pair of all-consuming addictions. I easily got a job as a manager of a women's clothing store—a job for which I was pathetically unsuited due to my hopeless lack of organizational and money-handling skills—and began to telegraph my single status to a growing following of eager men. Alcohol brought out and displayed my wild side, and I was eagerly flirtatious and seductive around them. At some point, a teacher from the very staid and proper Miss Porter's School for Girls in nearby

Farmington invited me to join him and his wife in a sexual three-some designed to spice up his marriage. I declined for lack of interest, but it is clear that this bold offer was an indication that my behavior—fueled by alcohol—was sending out some strong signals.

Eulalia was now pushing me to find someone else to marry so that our family could rid itself of the taint of my divorce. And although I thought I was heartily ignoring her advice and enjoying the single life, within a short time after Adam's departure from our house, I was seriously dating someone whose drinking habits were, if anything, more firmly entrenched than mine. Our mutual attraction to alcohol was passionate, and right from the beginning everything we did together and every decision we made sprang from our overwhelming desire to have fun together and consume more alcohol.

Kris

You'll notice in Mom's telling of her story how often she refers to some-one who caused her pain, anger or sadness when she was young. I know she was lonely and sad as a child, but I begin to lose patience with the way she tried to blame everyone but herself for her unhappiness. Her psychiatrist and friends probably thought my grandparents had horns and reported directly to the devil. If I hadn't known them personally, I probably would think they were terrible people because of Mom's stories. The reality is that raising kids was different when Mom was young. Maybe she was a child who would respond much better to something like today's parenting with all its reliance on praise and confidence-building. Maybe she should have rebelled while she was still a kid. Possibly that would have helped her become stronger in her struggle to be independent of her mother. Instead, as an insecure and passive adult, rather than making her own decisions and asserting herself, she followed a different path in her search for happiness—alcohol.

Given her hypersensitivity to the 'crimes' her mother committed against her, wouldn't you think my mom might have gone overboard to help Hallie and me develop a strong sense of self when we were little? Hallie says she wanted to make her own boys feel safe because she never felt that way herself as a child. And I always tucked my kids in tight when they were little and told them how much I loved them because I wanted them to feel more secure than I ever did as a child.

Both my mom and dad were raised in homes with controlling par-ents, but as they became young adults, one might think they would have developed the guts to speak for themselves about who to marry and where to live, and not allow my grandmother to make those important decisions for them. Despite their inability to stand up to my grand-mother, my parents were both very self-centered people. They partied a lot and moved often to suit my mother's growing restlessness. Honestly, if I think about it, I wonder how often they even gave much thought to what was best for my sister and me. Given the frequent moves we made, no wonder I so desperately dreamed of one day having that perfect little house with a little wooden fence to keep my own kids safe. My mom was good to me and I loved her but when I read her story, I begin to see more clearly when things started to go wrong for our family. It was earlier than I had imagined—even before the drinking got completely out of control. Eventually, everyone in our family would pay the price for my mother's problems.

After my parents split, I found it really difficult to make any real friends but thankfully, I was surrounded by nice kids in the neighborhood and was automatically accepted by them, despite being afraid of my own shadow and not wanting to call attention to myself. A memory of how shy I was comes from kindergarten days. The class was saying the pledge of allegiance and I was too shy to say the words out loud, so the teacher thought I was being a mini-rebel and grabbed me by the arm and put me in the coat closet to punish me! Later, in third grade, I was quietly sitting in the middle of the class sucking on a sweater button while listening to someone sharing a story. Suddenly the button popped off the sweater and lodged in my throat! I was too afraid to raise my hand to get help so I sat there as still as I could, unable to get any air. I started to hit myself in the chest, trying not to disturb anyone and just as I was beginning to panic, the button dislodged and I swallowed it. Now, that is low self esteem!

Imagine learning that your father was abusive to your mother and that she could have lost your little sister because of his actions. Dad's temper must have been linked to his own unhappiness in marriage—or maybe it was that problem plus the alcohol. How can I fully grasp all the hurt my mom endured and the emptiness she felt being in a relationship she didn't want and which she tried—however passively— to avoid? Her telling of her story makes me painfully aware that the sadness and emptiness that has often consumed me was not much different than hers. Like Mom, my continuing lack of confidence and my own inability to speak up was a problem for many years.

Wow, did my world ever get turned upside-down at the ripe old age of four! Imagine, one day life seemed good and then the next thing, a big truck shows up in your driveway to take away many familiar family belongings. That was the day Hallie and I realized my dad was really leaving us! Didn't he love us any more? We watched from the glass front door while he packed the truck and then drove off and disappeared from our sight. No one prepared us for such a horrendous day!

How could our dad leave and not tell us where he was going? Why didn't my mom prepare me for this change in our lives? Thankfully, my sister Hallie was still there and I loved her dearly. I decided that I would protect her! Little did I know that not only would I be Hallie's protector, but within a few years, I would be the protector and substitute mom for three siblings still to come.

Not long after our father's departure, Mom married Ron, a man we barely knew—a bachelor who didn't know anything at all about kids. At their wedding, the alcohol was flowing and everyone seemed a bit crazy to me! The ceremony was held on my grandparents' patio with a close group of friends there to witness it. Mom wore a dress that looked to me like Swiss cheese because it had holes in it. Thank goodness she was so pretty—she passed off that dress beautifully! She seemed happy, or at least she put on a really good show. Hallie looked adorable and happy in all the pictures, but I looked like a mourner at a funeral. I refused to smile for any of the pictures because that's just how I felt.

Why couldn't I smile? And why couldn't I join my sister and cousins who were all running around having fun? I wanted to be free like them, to act crazy, climb trees and get dirty but I was afraid! Mom had never asked Hallie and me whether we were happy or okay with her new situation. And although I would soon come to love our stepfather, who we began to call Pop, I didn't know what to make of this loud, crazy-haired man who always had to be at the center of attention.

The reception was held at my new stepfather's big house which was perched on top of a cliff. Pop had been living there with some of his buddies. I kept looking past the house to the edge of the cliff. It scared the life out of me! My head was spinning with worry about someone having too much fun and falling over the edge. To give you an idea how high this cliff is, take a look at the cliffs people hang glide from— that's the way this cliff was. I asked myself why someone hadn't built a fence to protect people from falling over! As the party progressed, the adults became completely wasted on booze and some of Pop's friends grabbed him and Mom, plopped them into a truck, and drove them to the nearby lake. Of course I was terrified that the truck would go over the cliff. When they got to the lake, the drunks threw Mom and Ron off the dock. To me it looked as if the two of them were being launched into the lake like skipping stones. The adults were having a blast, but I was terrified and just waiting for it to be over so I could go home and feel safe.

Many years after that day, I thought I had learned from my mom's failures in her three marriages, my biological father's three marriages, and my stepfather's two marriages. I chose my husband-to-be mainly because he seemed so grounded and because he had wonderful family values. But the fact is we were very different people and we both came from families scarred by addiction. He had his own reservations about our different backgrounds and how they would play out in our own marriage but I assured him it would all work out just fine. I had plenty of doubts myself, but I was not willing to share my fears with anyone—and certainly not him. Was I any different from my mom? Was I too afraid to speak my mind? Was I too afraid to admit I might not be ready for marriage?

Whatever the insecurities I was feeling, I was excited about getting married and held onto the thought of having beautiful children and raising them in a safe and loving environment. I badly wanted people to know that although Jane's kids grew up in a highly dysfunctional family, we were still capable of becoming normal, functional adults. I had read plenty of books that reinforced how wonderful life would be once I fell in love, got married and had my own children. I had always dreamed of a happy marriage and told myself I would never turn into my mom and mess up like her. I had put up walls around me and didn't want to take advice from anyone. I wanted to be a good example for my younger siblings! I would put on a brave face to show them it was possible to be happy in marriage. How ironic this all seems now, long after my own marriage broke up.

When I look back on my own wedding, I remember that my mom was placed in a horrible position because by then everyone was treating her as the family drunk. She was sober then but she was still extremely fragile and no one trusted her to stay sober. My biological dad had re-married and his current wife was involved in organizing the day along with my stepfather's new wife. Both women wanted to put their stamp on the wedding and they had no intentions of consulting or communicating with my mother! I can't imagine how hard it must have been for my mom to put on a brave face, be walked up the aisle and then directed to a seat to be flanked by my dad and his new wife and my stepfather and his new wife. Looking back, if it weren't so humiliating for Mom, I'd say it was a comical scene from a movie. It makes me sweat to imagine how she must have been feeling.

Always the people pleaser myself, and not wanting to hurt any feelings, I let both my stepfather and biological dad walk me down the aisle. It seems appropriate now that my bridesmaids wore horrible floral draperies made into dresses because those hideous things set the tone for a wedding which I had no part in planning and which I realize was terribly humiliating for my mother.

Thirteen years of marriage later, I was dying inside and miserably unhappy; but if you were to ask how I felt, it was always the same answer—fine. Well, the facade finally broke and I could no longer pretend that my life was okay. Everyone had thought I had a good marriage; it was the way our community viewed my mom's marriages! But the difference was that I wasn't drinking and trying to escape, although there were times when I was sorely tempted. My mom had ended her first marriage without saying a word to Hallie and me. I could at least claim to have been honest with my kids. I faced my young children and told them the truth about the impending divorce. It was painful to watch them shut down and cry themselves to sleep, but I knew it had to be done and I was the one who had to do it.

CHAPTER FIVE

☺

"I get juiced on Mateus and just hang loose."
—*Elton John, "Social Disease"*

Kris and Hallie stood in the doorway wistfully waving goodbye to their dad as he pulled away from our house in a loaded U-haul truck, but they did not fully comprehend that he would not be returning to us. The very next day, I went to a cocktail party in full single girl mode and met a fun-loving guy named Wallace Ronald. Ron had a full head of dark wavy hair and was wearing a loud, preppy tie which gave me something to make wry remarks about to get the sparks flying between us. He was a successful lumber broker and was in the process of transferring to Connecticut from Boston. Amazingly, he was still single and not in a committed relationship. He had a lot of energy and a bubbling, energetic personality. I noticed with interest that he was never at a loss for a party to go to or a new friend to win over. Best of all, he was a prodigious drinker who loved the company of other drinkers. I was swept into his vortex immediately and our exciting new relationship made me forget my goal to stay single forever.

In the early days of our relationship, our life together was all about drinking. I remember being so hung over after one of our ski weekends that I could only stop the shaking by drinking all the booze I kept hidden in my coat. Ron fell for me completely and within six months of our meeting, asked me to marry him. I eagerly accepted. In the days leading up to our marriage, I recall a day when I ran out of alcohol and remembered there was a case of Mateus in the house which had been a gift to Ron from a friend. It was not the sort of wine Ron would have selected and he had set it aside and forgotten about it. But when I was alone in the place and there was no other alcohol to drink, I went back to that case time and time again. One day, while looking for something else, Ron noticed with some surprise that most of the bottles in the Mateus case were missing and casually asked, "Jane, do you know what happened to the Mateus? I know we haven't been drinking it." I turned to him and answered simply with a lowered voice, "I think I'm an alcoholic."

With this simple statement, I had put Ron on notice that I was in trouble. But he quickly brushed aside my concerns and said reassuringly to me, "When we get married, things are going to get better." If this was a prediction of our future together, he couldn't have been further off the mark. I passively accepted his upbeat prediction, and reassured by his remarks, continued to try to keep up with his prodigious alcohol consumption. But alcohol is a form of insanity, and in my affair with it, I was on my way to becoming a mad woman.

Not surprisingly, I deferred to Ron's benign but controlling nature and found safety in his devotion to alcohol and partying. Ron got along well with my father, and the two often lifted glasses together and talked of hunting and fishing. But Ron and Eulalia circled each other uneasily right from the beginning, neither of them trusting the other. Ron was always uncomfortable with and suspicious of Eulalia's control over me and she was never willing to back off and allow him to become my new keeper. The rocky relationship between them was in constant further decline during our marriage and finally bottomed out when the two began trading nasty accusations in writing about who was responsible for my alcoholism and my inability to handle my adult responsibilities.

Despite the underlying natural tension between Ron and Eulalia, we were married at my parents' house; our fallback choice after the little Episcopal Church we had chosen refused to marry a divorced woman. Our wedding took place on a very hot summer day after a previous night's revelry when I stayed up all night drinking enormous quantities of champagne with a friend. I was so badly hung over on the morning of the ceremony that I needed a stiff drink to clear my head and stop the shakes. It seems that I was relying on those stiff drinks to prepare me for almost everything now. The snapshots of our wedding day reveal the puffiness in my face and remind me of the uncomfortable bloated feeling I had been experiencing regularly because of my serial drinking bouts and bulimic eating habits.

Ron and I had a short honeymoon in the Catskills, during which we drank constantly. Then, after returning to a house we had purchased in West Hartford, I became pregnant right away with my third and Ron's first biological child, Lindsey. Ron was very excited about the pregnancy and, at the same time, unfailingly loving and generous to both of my girls from my marriage to Adam. He never wanted to take Adam's place as their father, and asked the girls to call him Pop instead of Dad so that they would never forget who their real father was. But as time went on and Adam failed to demonstrate any consistent fatherly interest in them—he once told Ron casually and without shame that he had come to think of himself as more like an uncle to them—it became clear that they considered Ron to be their father and always would. After all, he was the one who supported them financially as well as emotionally—as a father would.

In the beginning of our marriage, while the girls were very young, I became a teacher's aide on the strength of my associate's degree in Early Childhood Education. Having that job and earning a paycheck gave me a feeling of pride that I had never experienced before. I was earning a pittance in the job, but the money was unimportant; I just loved the feeling for the first time of having a responsible job and doing it well. But in time, as my life became more chaotic and alcohol robbed me of any new self respect I might have developed, my sense of personal failure trumped the feeling of pride in working, and I quit.

As had happened twice before, I loved being pregnant and stopped drinking while carrying Lindsey. And when she was born, I found joy in the smell of a new baby, the closeness, and the feeling of being needed in such an elemental way. I even looked forward to getting up in the night to nurse my baby; these were the quiet times of my day, and often the happiest. But I didn't realize that the mix of additional childcare, the never-ending household chores, and our constant partying was taking a serious toll on me. Within sixth months of Lindsey's birth, I became pregnant again; this time, with my fourth child, Courtney.

Then, after less than two years in our house, I became restless again and wanted a change of venue. I told Ron I hated the fact that our house was surrounded by insurance executives' and doctors' houses. To me, the neighborhood was stilted and stuffy; an unpleasant reminder of the neighborhood and gigantic house Eulalia had chosen to entomb us in when I was growing up.

Ron—who was by now very well-connected and social in Hartford—was happy living in that neighborhood, but recognized my wanderlust and described it to friends as, "Jane's need to move, move, move, move." And so, when Courtney's arrival made it clear that we had physically grown out of our house, I started looking for the perfect place for our family. Ultimately, I found a large, handsome Georgian brick house on a hill overlooking the city of Hartford. The house had been built on the 100-year-old property of a Vanderbilt family summer home on West Hill that had been torn down—an unwanted Victorian manse—without ever being lived in. Previously, the brick house built in its place along with several other houses had been the home to two other families with children and needed a lot of work on its large public rooms, kitchen and many bedrooms and baths. But I loved the feel of the place and its wonderful old woodwork. To my restless mind, the hassle of renovation would be worth it! Ron was initially skeptical, but when he saw the house, he liked it as much as I did, and soon we were committed to a major renovation. It was during our chaotic transition and rebuilding orgy that Tyler—my fifth child and our only son—was born.

Ron was an energetic businessman and added the title of restaurant owner to his résumé in addition to the wood brokering business in which he was already very successful. Understandably, he was increasingly away from home during most of our waking weekday hours, and I was left to manage the household and children alone. After Lindsey's birth, I had once more picked up where I left off with the drinking, and now I became a vodka-fueled June Cleaver! In one pathetic attempt to stop drinking on my own, after an endless day in which I managed to avoid alcohol completely, I sat alone on the carpeted floor—my legs rubbery, my hands trembling—and wept freely. I realized that this do-it-your-self attempt was not going to work; I simply could not get sober on my own. I was a complete fuck-up. Even my tears tasted like vodka. In that moment, I felt the first pangs of the hopelessness and despair that would be my constant companion for many years to come. I couldn't even look at myself in the mirror. I knew what I would see; dirty, unkempt hair, puffy face, glassy eyes—that person couldn't be me, could she?

I had resumed my courses at the University of Hartford and was getting reasonably good grades, but now the drinking was getting in the way of that too. I enjoyed the lively exchange of ideas in a university environment which was new to me. I reveled in the attention I was getting from some of the professors who found me attractive and invited me for drinks after class. Their attentions toward me—in some cases overtly sexual—gave me the excitement and attention I craved. One night after one of these Happy Hour meetings with a professor, I was driving home tipsy in a vintage Jaguar which a developer friend had loaned to Ron in exchange for borrowing our rugged Suburban for a muddy tour of a new building site. Suddenly, I couldn't handle a curve and smashed into a lamppost. The Jaguar was still marginally drivable despite significant damage, so I was able to limp home in it and when I got there, I simply left the smoking, oil-dripping wreck out in our driveway and told Ron, "Sorry, I guess I wrecked the Jag on the way home. Slippery road! Can you handle this for me?" As far as I remember it, I was completely unaffected by the whole incident, cocooned as I was in my alcoholic comfort zone.

My drinking was getting dramatically worse until I finally decided to go in for treatment in an attempt to quiet the raging addiction beast inside me. Ron chose the program; a one-week, 12-step kind of program that took place in an old rickety farmhouse in Litchfield. In reality, it was just a dry-out and a rest from the children and there certainly was no follow-up family therapy. I am not sure Ron would have felt the need to participate even if there had been a family therapy component; he wanted me cured but didn't see a role for himself in achieving that. Like many spouses of that day and time, he never cancelled our plans for parties and socializing in order to help me stop drinking. In fact, after many of my treatment stays, I came home just when he was preparing for a cocktail party at our house that night. He just expected that the treatment had enabled me to stay sober and continued to do what he had always done—drink and party with friends.

I went to Beech Hill Hospital in New Hampshire four times in all. The first time was a relief—a getaway from the kids for 28 days—and it provided good food, group sessions, counseling, and a structure for my daily life which I was incapable of establishing for myself. Afterwards, I tried attending AA in a local church basement, but quickly became bored and found reasons to stop going. Within a month, I was drinking again, but more carefully. Now I was disguising my alcohol with various types of soda or juice.

The common rule in those days was that an alcoholic would get out of treatment, start going to AA, and get a sponsor. I didn't have any help with childcare at home, so going out to AA meetings would have been difficult but still possible if I had actively pursued the idea. However, I did not possess the kind of self discipline that was required to make a schedule, get the childcare help and then go to the meetings. Undoubtedly, doing so would have helped me. And I never went to a 3-month halfway house although it was often strongly recommended to me. I was just too overwhelmed at home, and there wasn't a good halfway house anywhere around. So my experience after coming home from treatment was a far cry from today's practice that is based on the notion that when a member of a family is struggling with addiction, each member of the family needs to help and be helped.

When a couple is a drinking couple, the whole dynamic changes because one of the two is trying to stay sober. In effect, because you are drinking buddies, you can't have fun together if one of you is sober. And in my case, when I was sober, I felt shy and reserved and wanted to be alone. When I was drunk, I was a flirtatious extrovert—the life of the party. In the throes of my addiction, I simply wasn't strong enough to resist the need to be that lively, popular extrovert. Looking back, I am not so sure I could have stayed sober even if Ron had stayed sober himself. But maybe I would have had a fighting chance.

Ron was the party animal and I was his eager partner as long as I was anesthetized with alcohol. Our house had become the go-to house for parties and we were the fun, welcoming hosts. Everyone wanted to befriend us. By now, I was having secret morning drinks to get myself going. At the same time, I was immersed in the country club sports of tennis and paddle tennis and began to win tournaments regularly. Despite the appearance of such outwardly healthy pursuits, I always carried a small bottle of Smirnoff in my gym bag and frequently fortified myself with a few nips right there on the court between sets. Who needs Gatorade when there is alcohol in your gym bag?

I started running in some 5K races despite the inevitable hangovers that I awoke with on race mornings. But somehow I could still run and do well. I did make occasional attempts to stop drinking and when I did, my other addiction—bulimia—was there to soothe me in the absence of the alcohol that had been performing that vital function. When I was drinking, I essentially went without eating. But when I was not drinking, the bulimia gave me a way to eat a lot and then make myself feel good by throwing up. I was becoming a master at using my twin addictions to cope with anxiety and the chaotic feelings that roiled my insides.

Ron had genuine friends. I had acquaintances, but no close friends except vodka and champagne. I loved them both dearly and just the thought of not having them in my life scared me to death. It just wasn't an option. If I didn't have those two friends, who would comfort me and make me feel happy? Who would make me feel alive? Loved? By now, I had no idea who I would or could be as a sober person. My mother's opinion of me—that I was never quite good enough or smart enough—seemed to be all I had to go on. Vodka and champagne made me feel good; they helped me forget her voice, her words. With those two friends, I could fool anyone into thinking I was whoever they thought I was. Someone smart and lively? Sure, why not? I really had no idea. But the problem with having friends like vodka and champagne was that they made me really self-centered. I was beginning to hurt people—especially Ron and my innocent children.

As an alcoholic, my tolerance for alcohol was high and I could handle enormous quantities of it without throwing up like a frat house binge drinker. How ironic it seems now that as a bulimic, I found comfort in bingeing and then throwing up. In the worst of my darkest period—which was still ahead of me—I could drink a fifth of vodka in one night without throwing up, passing out, or dying of alcohol poisoning. Of course, I frequently ended up in hospitals on an IV, but I was still alive. I have a genetically strong constitution. Other people die of such extreme amounts of alcohol, but I often drank straight out of the bottle; often while alone behind the wheel of my car. When I was out with my children, I routinely added alcohol to the orange juice or Diet Coke in a plastic cup from a fast food place which I carried with me at all times.

After Tyler's birth I went right back into the heavy drinking. It isn't easy for anyone to have five young children and a large house with little help for cooking and cleaning. But for me, especially in my compromised condition, it was completely overwhelming. While I give Ron all the credit in the world for the kind of father he became for my children, it was also true that, like my father, he had very little involvement with the children when they were little. His job was to make a living outside our house. Sick as I was with my addictions, I just kept trying to be a hands-on mom and handle things myself.

Ron had slowly progressed in his attitude toward my drinking problem from a state of benign denial to what seemed to me like intolerance and fury, so I became skilled at hiding empties and new bottles alike. In fact, I was quite adept at going to neighbors' houses and asking to borrow a bottle of vodka is if it were a cup of sugar! I rang the doorbell, and when someone answered, I simply said, "Gosh, sorry, but we've got unexpected guests today and we've run out of vodka. Could I borrow a bottle from you and replace it tomorrow?" At first, my unsuspecting neighbors had no idea that I was the only guest at my party! It was an unbelievably cheeky thing to do, and I can't imagine what they thought when I pulled this little gambit on them more than once. In any case, I always made short work of the borrowed vodka, and never replaced any of it. Alcoholism does that to you. The sincere thanks and the promises to replace what you borrowed are all part of the bullshit you spew on a daily basis.

Ron was a functioning drinker; I was not. I remember some scenes from the early days of our marriage that could have been taken directly from the Jack Lemmon classic film, *The Days of Wine and Roses*. As our marriage and the drinking continued, I was drinking both wine and vodka in attempt to slake my alcoholic thirst. Alcohol was an important part of Ron's life, but unlike me, he could function quite well even when he had ingested a lot of it. He could just get up the next day, do a long run or rake the lawn or do exercises until he felt better. But he could also be very controlling—especially when he was drinking— and I don't engage well when people are telling me what to do. I had enough of that when I was a child taking orders from Eulalia.

Ron enabled my drinking for a long time and we co-existed in the state of enabler-drinker quite well, but when he began locking up the alcohol and hiding it from me, I rebelled. Once he went into the restaurant business, it was inevitable that he would have an extensive wine and spirits collection in the house. I remember a particular Sunday when I had run out of my stash of hidden bottles because Ron knew where they all were and had disposed of them. In Connecticut, the ancient Blue Laws prevented purchasing alcohol on Sunday. Chances are that I had already run out my string with borrowing booze from the neighbors. In any case, on that particular Sunday, I found myself out of options and staring at the locked door of Ron's wine collection in the basement.

I shouldn't have been surprised that he had the collection in lockdown, but this brash sign of his distrust insulted and irritated me. Whatever my confused reactions were, I didn't dwell on those thoughts for long and quickly came up with a way to foil Ron's strategy. I rustled around the basement until I found a crowbar, and with a considerable amount of grunting and muscle flexing, managed to tear the padlocked door completely off its hinges, leaving it hanging only by a padlock, like a loose tooth dangling by its pulp. At this point in my descent into hell, I was single-minded and undaunted when it came to getting what I wanted. Looking back, I see how pathetic and desperately lost I was.

I was beginning to hate sex. If I wasn't drinking, the intimacy and the act itself seemed almost intolerable to me. If I was drunk, I could tolerate it. Somehow sex had developed for me simply as a way to appease a man. I can only guess that this was a notion that grew from that strange sexual encounter with my brother when I was eight. As an adult, I found that the act itself evolved as a way for me to get something from a man. The sex was my affectionate *thank you* for whatever he had relinquished to me. And in some instances, sex was my way of keeping a relationship smooth—a peace exchange. I had evolved ways to use sex as a magical tool with which to manipulate a man and thereby feel a measure of emotional and physical control amidst a chaotic life. I did not feel a sense of intimacy with my partner; I had never felt that in the past and now I felt even more strongly detached.

I did a lot of drunk driving in those days and usually managed to cover it up. But one day when I was getting ready for a party at our house, I stopped to pick up an order at the fish market and left my two littlest children, Tyler and Courtney, in the car alone. I must have drunkenly left the car in neutral, because it rolled backward and crashed into a wall. Miraculously, the children were unhurt and I calmly continued to drive the car after that near miss. But then I hit a man on a bike—all in less than an hour! The injured biker later sued Ron for damages. Ron took care of everything like that.

It is hard to believe, but I guess I thought I had been hiding my drunkenness pretty effectively. I didn't know the kids were so focused on my erratic and unpleasant behavior, or that Ron, although tolerating more than most people would, would finally have his own moment of truth as he describes below.

> **Ron:** For the most part, Jane covered up her drunkenness in those days and I only saw her out of control once in the 1970's. I was scheduled to take her to a clinic the next day, but the night before that I was going to a hockey game with a friend. When I got home after the game, she was passed out cold on the couch in the family room hugging an empty bottle of vodka the way a child hugs a stuffed bear. In my memory, that was the only time she appeared to me to be out of control. I was angry and took a Polaroid picture of her that way. When she woke up, I showed her the picture and challenged her: "Is this the way you want the children to see you?"

I became pregnant for a sixth time when my drinking was at this new, very intense stage and or the first time I was uncertain about being pregnant. I knew that being pregnant meant that I would have to be sober and healthy, but my alcoholism had progressed enough to make me question whether I could stop drinking for nine months. As much as I had always loved the feeling of being pregnant, I had begun to love the feelings associated with drinking even more. Ron and my doctors knew that I was not in any condition to have another baby. They agreed that both my mental and physical health—and presumably that of the baby—would be severely challenged with a sixth pregnancy. Dr. Howard told me bluntly what I already suspected, "You simply can't continue to have babies while you are in such a self-destructive state." Of course, Eulalia forced herself into the conversation and briefly stepped out of her denial about my drinking to make the pronouncement that there was no way I could handle a sixth child. For the first time ever, Eulalia and Ron had agreed on something! Ultimately, I made the decision to have an abortion. But as soon as I made the decision, I felt the crushing weight of failure. For a long time, my entire identity had been wrapped up in my motherhood, and now I saw that—along with everything else in my life—I had screwed that up too.

On the day of the abortion, Ron dropped me off at the hospital with my little overnight bag and told me he would pick me up the next morning. I had never felt so alone and emotionally destitute as I did then. Not surprisingly, very soon after the abortion, I found myself plunged in the bottomless hole of a very deep, unmovable depression. Ron was powerless to fix this frightening new problem and depended on Dr. Howard to help me. Early anti-depression meds were just being introduced at that time, and Dr. Howard prescribed some for me. But the drugs made me groggy and caused me to gain unwanted weight. So I abandoned them and started drinking again with a vengeance.

When I told Dr. Howard about how much I had been drinking and described incidents in which I had been hiding bottles and borrowing liquor from the neighbors, he again sent me to the 28-day program at Beech Hill Hospital in Dublin, New Hampshire. I was to return two more times to Beech Hill in the next couple of years, but my addiction was so entrenched that each time I came home and once again became overwhelmed by my family duties, it was only a few days until I started drinking again.

I began to see Dr. Howard regularly and he asked to meet my parents. When he interviewed Eulalia, she took the opportunity to blame Ron for most of my problems. Dr. Howard recognized that both my parents were in a great deal of denial about many of our family problems—including those of my brothers—and observed that they were especially out of touch with my situation. When we were alone again, he identified my mother as the center of the family's difficulties. This is when he gave me the rationalization I was seeking when he referred to my mother by saying, "No wonder you drink." He later commented further that my mother's controlling nature and the way she treated me like a child was a major contributing factor in my struggle with alcohol. But Eulalia remained in open and aggressive denial about possible sources of my situation. When pressed to admit that I had a problem, she insisted on blaming it on Ron. I had no idea what my father's view of my problem was. He never talked to me about it—or, in fact, anything else that mattered.

It was hard for me to maintain sobriety when our house was full of liquor and our social life was based on drinking. I don't blame him for this any more, but Ron's lack of support certainly didn't help; he thought that paying for my treatment should suffice and did not see any need to support my struggle by giving up his own relationship with alcohol. In the meantime, I had began to rely more and more on my little girl Kris—who was only about 12 at the time—to help with our other children. It was a terrible arrangement—and totally unfair to Kris. Using her as my backup, I began to go to Beech Hill and other treatment centers regularly for longer stays, but with little effect.

I was a model subject in the treatment centers. I followed all the rules, participated passively in all the mindless handicrafts sessions, made no trouble, and said all the right things to manipulate the treatment staffs and line them up on my side. But when I got home and became immersed again in my chaotic life, I always relapsed quickly and painfully. Ron's father had died of alcoholism, and his mother had gone to Alanon to learn about the disease in the 1950s when there was not much informed public information about alcoholism and very little in the way of family support systems. His family had talked openly about the disease, but somehow he lost the notion of such an enlightened approach when I was the alcoholic in question. On the other hand, his mother was a very understanding person and loved me in spite of my messy problems. In fact, she became my strongest supporter and advocate after everyone else had essentially given up on me.

In the grip of the depression that took hold after my abortion, I began for the first time to have fantasies about leaving my family. I felt intensely guilty about this kind of thinking, but always assured myself that my motives were pure and I often rationalized that I could be cured if I could just get away from all the pressures and duties of my family life. While I was enumerating my twisted version of virtuous reasons for leaving, my 'escape brain' began to work actively on the idea that leaving would be an exciting new start to my life; a single, unencumbered life. I even thought about where I might live. I knew that Ron owned some condos in Amherst, Massachusetts and decided I could live in one of them while working on my recovery. Then I talked Dr. Howard into the idea, telling him disingenuously, "Living in Amherst will give me the rest I need from my family life in order to stop drinking. I can come back on weekends in better shape for the kids. I can be a better mother and wife if I get some time to myself." Thus convinced by such a crudely manipulative presentation, the doctor began to believe that this could be a possible cure for my out-of-control addiction. Looking back, it seems ridiculously naïve of him, but I had become a master at getting what I wanted.

And so, with Dr. Howard's support, and Ron's sad compliance, I left my family to live on my own in Amherst, Massachusetts to "work on overcoming my addictions." At the time, Kris was 14, Hallie was 11, Lindsey was 6, Courtney was 5, and Tyler was only 3. I did not imagine then that this would become a permanent arrangement. And I did not realize—or maybe I wasn't capable of facing my deepest motives—that with the decision to leave home, I had become a member of that small, reviled company of mothers who abandon their innocent children to pursue their own messy lives.

Coincidentally, in that same year—1979—an Academy Award-winning movie called *Kramer vs. Kramer* stunned movie audiences with its raw look at an unhappy mother who leaves her husband and very young son in an attempt to find herself. The movie disturbed me when I first saw it and I thought immediately, "This is *my* story!" as I empathized with Meryl Streep's portrayal of Joanna Kramer, the unhappy mother. I have tried, but have never been able to watch the movie again. The feelings it stirred in me so long ago were too wrenchingly painful to bear repeating. While listening to Joanna's self-loathing justifications for leaving her small son, I was overwhelmed with sorrow and remorse about my own situation. I played with those same kinds of excuses in my own life, but unlike Joanna Kramer's situation, my addiction had devoured me and I simply had no clue how to become a mature woman with a productive future. The sad truth is, I was leaving my family so that I could drink myself into oblivion without interruption or intervention. I adopted a new self-justifying mantra: *Ron and the kids will be better off without me.*

So I packed my bags into the back seat of my Honda and after the unspeakable, disingenuous goodbyes, drove to Amherst with the tape player cranked up to its loudest decibel level and tears flowing freely while I belted out the title song from a movie called "It's My Turn" starring Jill Claybourgh:

I can't cover up my feelings in the name of love
Or play it safe for a while that was easy
And if living for my self is what I'm guilty of

Go on and sentence me I'll still be free
It's my turn
To see what I can see

I hope you'll understand
This time's just for me
Because it's my turn
With no apologies

I've given up the truth
To those I've tried to please
But now it's my turn

If I don't have all the answers
At least I know
I'll take my share of chances

Ain't no use in holding on
When nothing stays the same
So I'll let it rain '
Cause the rain ain't gonna hurt me

And I'll let you go
Though I know it won't be easy
It's my turn
With no more room for lies

For years I've seen my life
Through someone else's eyes
And now it's my turn

To try and find my way
And if I should get lost
At least I'll own today

It's my turn
Yes, it's my turn.

> *Lyrics by Michael Masser and Carole Bayer Sager, from the movie "It's My Turn"*

I adored this song because it gave me a glimmer of an idea about the person I might become. I wanted to invent a better image of myself and fantasized that by moving to a new place with none of the baggage of a young, needy family, I could shed the past and create a stronger more authentic person. I would simply disown the old me! Unfortunately, when I arrived in Amherst and unpacked my stuff, out of the suitcases came my old self with all the weakness, failure, guilt and torment—and, of course, the full-blown drinking problem.

Kris

This chapter is disturbing and hurtful; first, it hurts to learn that my mother was so quick to turn around and look for another guy right after my dad left. She put herself out there to meet someone new the very next day! How could she have simply ignored the signs that Hallie and I were suffering after seeing our father leave? Was she so selfish that she didn't care about anyone but herself? Apparently she was!

Then there is Mom claiming that she told Ron about her alcoholism before they married. Was this just another of her attempts to be a victim and blame Ron for not taking her seriously when she asked for help? His story differs from hers:

Ron: Jane thinks she said something to me before we married about her drinking being a problem. But I can't imagine that I thought being married would cure anyone's drinking problem. Truthfully, I had not seen anything dysfunctional about her drinking, even long after we were married. After all, Jane won the women's doubles championship right here in West Hartford and ran a road race several times. She didn't even have to train for these things. She was a natural! Maybe I was so in love with her that I overlooked her growing drinking problem, but I never saw her being violent or out of control. When it came out that Jane was an alcoholic, people in Hartford were aghast. They hadn't seen it either. It was later, when we had all five kids, that it became more obvious to everyone.

Then there is that story about Mom driving home in the borrowed Jag. It was so like her to leave her messy problems to someone else. Ron adored her and was always willing to pick up the pieces for her, even after their marriage was over and he was with another woman.

Ron: That particular night it was raining and I believe it was in the fall when the leaves made driving conditions slippery. I think Jane was coming from a class at University of Hartford and I know the 45-degree turn she needed to make on the hill and can understand how it happened as she accelerated and the car spun out. I don't believe that I attributed the accident to drinking since the circumstances of weather made it plausible that it happened as it did. Let me say that Jane was the master of disguise and she hid her drinking very well and it was not obviously visible. But now I wonder if she was even coming home from a class...

Now, about the "It's My Turn" scene in which Mom is singing at the top of her lungs the most selfish song I can imagine. I can understand her singing this if she was just getting away from a man and an unhappy or abusive marriage. But this is her saying good-bye to five kids who are lost and confused and devastated that their mother is leaving! Just the thought of this song will forever piss me off because I associate it with the messed-up selfish thinking of someone who wants to forget about everything and move forward without looking back at the destructive wake she is churning up behind her. Alcoholics are unbelievably self-centered people; they can't see past their own needs! Mom couldn't see what was happening to her children because of the alcohol, but to my mind, she had everything she ever needed in order to make a happy life and still she couldn't make it work! I know she had it tough growing up and endured some ugly episodes in her life, but what makes her so special and different from the legions of people with problems and issues who understand that running away and starting a new life isn't an option?

My mom was so weak; it's still really unbelievable to me that she left all of us. I am not saying that she was in the perfect marriage but when a person decides to bring children into the world, everything changes. Decisions are based on what is best for the kids. Normal people work with what they have. You bring children into this world; you have the responsibility to make sure you take care of them! I am no saint and I am not a perfect mother but I could never, ever imagine not being there to help and guide my kids while they are growing up. My younger siblings know painfully well what it feels like to be on a playing field or a stage and look out into the crowd to see if your mom is watching and then realize that once again she is not there. Often she wasn't there because she forgot she had promised to be there or she was so drunk she couldn't even get off her couch. My siblings know what it is like to look forward to a weekend visit with my mom, pack their suitcases, wait for her endlessly, and then finally realize she isn't going to show up.

I find it interesting that Mom saw herself as the mother in *Kramer vs. Kramer*. I don't see the resemblance. When I saw the movie, I cried for the little boy and his father, but not for Joanna. She had different issues from Mom's; being a drunk was not one of them.

In those difficult years, I tried to keep my anger, hurt and frustration to myself but it was tearing me apart. When Hallie and I were little and my dad was still around, we knew my mom was fully present for us and we felt her love. But my younger siblings, born after Mom married Ron, were robbed of the feelings of safety and warmth that a mother can give! It pains me to think of how I tried to replace my mom when she left. I didn't even know who I was! I was just an unformed teenager who didn't have a clue how to fill a loving mother's shoes. Thankfully, I had the memories of who my mom was before all the alcohol and craziness. Those memories helped me provide an approximation of a motherly role model for the younger kids. But I still regret that Hallie was left to fend for herself because I was so consumed by my efforts to be a mom to the little ones after our mother abandoned us.

Mom hid in her room a lot after having the abortion. She was really depressed over having made this decision. In my mind, this is when things really started to change for good. I wonder if my mom ever cuddled with the younger ones or made them feel safe. If Hallie didn't feel safe, then how could the younger ones feel any better? Lindsey, Courtney and Tyler were so quiet growing up; well, not Lindsey, but Courtney and Tyler. They were such good kids and didn't push the boundaries when they were young. I loved them so and wanted them to feel loved.

I will never forget the day I was playing with Courtney and threw her up in the air on my parents' bed one morning and she landed funny! She screamed and I tried to hold her and make her feel better, but she was inconsolable. My mom screamed at me for what I had done and ordered me to go to school. Later in the day, the teacher called me to her desk and told me that my sister had broken her leg and would be in the hospital. Can you imagine how I felt? I was the one who had broken her leg! I got home from school and my parents insisted that I be taken down to the hospital to see what I had caused. My sister, tiny and with big soft brown eyes lay in a bed in a body cast all the way up to her waist. I was distraught. I told myself that I would never let any of my siblings get hurt again.

Hair brushing, baths, making ponytails and tucking my siblings into bed were my specialties while Mom was still at home. I saw how much those little kids loved Mom and always wanted to make her happy. They couldn't see that she was becoming resentful towards all her responsibilities as a mother because they were taking her away from her first love; drinking. Alcoholism is a god-awful disease that pulls a person away from everything and everyone they love and cherish. Maybe it is best that Mom doesn't know in detail everything she missed.

On special school occasions, I was the one who went to lunch with the little kids when they were in elementary school. I am the one who walked with them to the park on the weekends so they could run around and play on the jungle gym. I was the one who went to class presentations when the two youngest were in a Montessori school. To me, this kind of participation in their lives was the new normal.

Mom must have been getting more and more desperate while her drinking problem began to explode. But she was very good at turning off the emotional gauge and pretending everything was normal! The sad thing is that some of her messed-up coping skills were rubbing off on me. Years later my husband would wonder how I could seemingly dismiss problems and move on as if they never happened. At an early age I had learned from Mom that it was easier to avoid looking back and dwelling on problems or the might-have-beens. Like her, I just kept looking forward to the next thing.

After my mom married Pop and the two of them went on to have three more children, life seemed basically normal to me for awhile. But I began to notice my mom doing a lot of odd things like not being able to remember where she parked her car. And then there were all those *times I have mentioned when she became cranky and snappy around dinner time. I became aware of many other things not being right. My mom was the queen of creativity when it came time to hiding the alcohol bottles. I started finding empty bottles in everything from the washing machine to the bread box. And Pop was getting calls from a liquor store where they knew him; they wanted him to know how often she was buying booze and how much. Mom thought she was fooling everyone, but Hallie, Lindsey and I already saw clearly what was happening:*

Hallie: Kris has a steel trap memory and remembers everything that happened with our mother, but I tend to remember incidents that were particularly troublesome. For instance, I remember the day—perhaps when I was in second grade—when I went to feed the dogs and found a liter of vodka in the dry dog kibble. I asked Mommy about it and she started screaming at me and berating me saying over and over; "Who told you to feed the dogs?!"

I remember being very confused and telling Pop what happened. Then he told me for the first time that Mommy was an alcoholic. Now I was confused even more. *What was an alcoholic?*

I was on a trip with a friend when she told me her mother told her that my mother had a drinking problem. I had just thought that is the way Mom was. Pop must have been protecting us and hiding the problem. But we certainly knew something was not right. I would be setting the table and she would yell at me, "Put the fork on the correct side!" Then she would yell something like, "Put your thinking cap on!" She did that a lot. It made me feel stupid and ashamed.

When her drinking became so much worse, I remember thinking her hair looked greasy. I had always thought she was so beautiful and now I wondered why she didn't keep herself looking pretty like the other moms did. And I wondered why she didn't bother to wear underwear.

My children feel secure and loved. I never felt safe. I was scared of my mother's unpredictable behavior because I had learned that she could get really mean quickly. In fact, my worst, most terrifying memory of how quickly my mother could change while drinking is never far from my consciousness.

Ron and his new wife had wanted some 'alone time' and sent me to Mom's place for the weekend. I have no idea what they did with the little kids, but I know they were not with me. Thank goodness. That weekend, Mom got really plastered and started laying into me, calling me names and telling me I was stupid. This went on for a while until I got into bed and tried to pretend I was asleep to get her leave me alone. But Mom still came into the room and got into my face, screaming, "Pay attention to me! I may be dead by morning!" Those words are permanently burned into my memory.

Lindsey: Once there was a policeman at school who was giving a safety presentation to the kids. Without really thinking about it, I remember going up to him—crying—and telling him that my mother was an alcoholic.

Here's the thing, it wasn't just alcohol that was a problem; Mom was also bulimic. Hallie and I began to notice that stuff like coffee cake and gooey éclairs was often missing. Stuff that had been there when we went to bed was mysteriously gone in the morning when we wanted it for breakfast. Eventually, Hallie and I figured out she was purging because often we couldn't stand to use the bathroom after Mom filled it with the smell of vomit. Hallie and I would roll our eyes at each other after Mom purged. Sometimes, all I could think was, What a waste of good food! Eventually, I started to hide some of the bakery goodies and sweets Mom brought home from the store and became a closet eater myself.

Mom's idea of cooking and cleaning was kind of sad. She was obsessed with keeping the kitchen clean and often stayed up late to make sure every dish was put away and the counters cleaned. She rotated four different menus, cooking them over and over again. Unfortunately, when she was cooking for us, she made only enough food for three people when there were five kids' mouths to feed. Instead of complaining, I was using the snacks I sneaked so I could fill up before dinner because I knew there wouldn't be enough to eat during the meal. I wasn't consuming and then purging huge amounts of food to chase away unhappiness the way Mom did; I was sneaking stuff like ice cream, candy bars and other sweet treats because I was actually hungry!

When Mom wasn't around, I cooked for my siblings. When I cooked, I made burgers in the McDonalds' style along with French fries and milkshakes. I don't know if they remember my cooking but I remember that our meals together were fun for us because everything was much more relaxed when mom wasn't present. When she was there, we could feel the tension radiating from her. In those years, there was a certain tone in her voice; I eventually learned that it was a voice inside her screaming out to escape from us so she could drink.

Why was I the one who was always around when things went wrong? Why wasn't Mom paying attention to the younger ones? She should have been aware that Courtney was running around holding a flute cleaning rod when she was a toddler. As Courtney tripped and tumbled forward, she opened her mouth and the metal tool pierced a hole through the back of her throat. That wound healed up faster than the wound caused when our dog attacked Courtney in the kitchen just moments before my parents headed out to a party. The dog's claw sliced Courtney across the throat and cut her face (inches from her eye). After a few accidents like that, I began to realize that I needed to be fully in charge of my younger siblings. If I didn't watch out over them, who else would? I haven't even mentioned the amount of times I jumped in to save one of them from the bottom of a pool, or Lindsey from falling backwards into the lit fireplace as we all stood there while family pictures were being taken.

Pop would come home from work and Mom would stiffen up. You could tell that he wanted her attention as much as we did, and he would try to give her a kiss or hug and there was no emotion in her body language at all. Maybe she is just tired, I told myself, but her body language spoke volumes. Sadly enough, I started to think men were undesirable or dirty because of Mom's behavior and I greatly suffered for that when I was first introduced to boys. I didn't know how to act around them. I really had no one to turn to other than my cousin Liz, who was my rock growing up. In my imagination and through all the books I read, I imagined love would be powerful and affectionate. But I didn't have a good sense of what a healthy relationship was about. There were times when Mom and Pop seemed to have fun together, but it became more apparent as I got older that much of that impression was because Mom was in her happy drinking mode.

At some point, my mom would return from her short stints in a rehab facility and seem to hold her own for a bit. But even sober, Mom had the patience of a gnat. She would snap about something, lose her ability to cope, and then relapse! I guess she always decided it was better to go back to alcohol because she could only maintain her happy disposition while drinking. Everyone loved her, and people thought we had the perfect life; big house, wonderful trips, healthy kids, great social life! You never know what goes on behind closed doors.

I have often wondered what I would have been like if the circumstances of my upbringing had been different. Would I have been more confident? Would I have been more successful in business? Or was I destined to be the same person I have become? I have no doubt that I learned a great deal from my childhood and it wasn't all bad. But at an important period, Mom was spinning out of control and I was watching, powerless, from the sidelines. Today, I tell my fitness clients and my children that balance is important to a successful life. I often say, "I don't want to need something so badly that in order to survive, I have to quit it."

The relationship between Grandma Bartels and Pop was a tough one. I know she didn't want to accept any responsibility for what was going on with her daughter. But the part that was difficult for me after Mom left us was that Grandma started pressuring me to get information on Pop and tell her about anything that might be going on in the house. She would bribe me by buying me clothes and taking me out with her so she could pump me for any information she could use against him. Pop always stood his ground and handled her well by not giving her any information. It must have been hard for him; he had barely any time to figure out how he was going to survive with five kids with no mother, let alone deal with his crazy mother-in-law! I was always proud of how Pop took the higher ground and avoided feeding into my grandma's nonsense.

Once Pop was on his own, I knew that I was the best person to help him. I never questioned or ran from that role because it all seemed quite natural to me. After all, he hadn't abandoned Hallie and me. Instead he had included us as his own. I longed to support him in every way I could. Mom showed poor judgment by falling into a relationship with Pop immediately after my dad left. But still, I am grateful that she chose Pop; most men would have run from the responsibility of raising another man's two children, and later from dealing with all the other problems Mom brought into his life. My mother was blessed to have my stepfather picking up the pieces she left strewn throughout our family's life for so many years, even after they were divorced.

Pop took a little while to get used to having a family. But once he got into it, he did some amazing things that I will never forget. I remember when he took Hallie and me on a trip to Bermuda. We stayed in a small villa and Pop climbed the trees to grab coconuts to give to us. He was a lot of fun and never ran out of energy. Right from the beginning, Pop took it upon himself to give us what we began to call "Pop's Life Lessons." The first of these happened on that Bermuda trip. He wanted us to try different foods and I remember he persuaded me to try calf brain and cow tongue on that trip... not a fan! He took Hallie and me to a poor section of the island to show us how fortunate we were to be on a vacation like this while there were poor people living there with barely enough to live on.

Somewhere along the way, Hallie's and my father seemed to become more of an uncle and less of a father, while Pop supported us and acted like a good stepfather to us. Pop taught us how to ski and sail and continued with his many Life Lessons. We didn't always appreciate those lessons because he used them to get things done his way. For instance, there was no sitting around watching TV in our house. Pop kept us busy all the time. We were annoyed by this, but as an adult I appreciate what he was trying to do for us.

Pop adored my mom and supported her in whatever she needed. But unfortunately I don't think he saw how her disintegration by alcohol was taking its toll on us kids. I agree with Mom; there is nothing better than the smell of a young baby or the giggles that come from deep within a baby's belly. But on the flip side, she doesn't have to remember—as I do— the sadness and tears that came from my siblings after her departure.

It angers me to hear her tales of getting away with things like driving drunk with the kids in the car. That could have easily ended in tragedy. She was unbelievably lucky it didn't and I am just thankful that we all survived.

As a teenager, I was surprised to find that I could love anyone as strongly as I loved my siblings. Their pains and fears were never lost on me. I recall one summer weekend when I was instructed to drop the kids off at my mom's place so they could all go spend some time together at the beach. When we arrived, I saw that my mother was so drunk that she was incapable of forming a complete sentence. I made the instantaneous decision to leave her there in her stupor and take the kids to the beach myself. I recall thinking that Mom might die that weekend and that I did not even care if she did.

Like Mom, I had a horrible sense of direction and didn't really know where I was going, but I drove in the direction of the water and eventually, we got to a god-awful motel near a beach where we spent the night. The only thing in my head was that I was not going to let those kids down. I don't even know how I paid for the motel and food but at least we got through the weekend safely.

As time went on and Mom's drinking became truly frightening, it was time for me to go to college. The day of my departure for college will be embedded in my brain forever. I remember grabbing my bags to head to the Hartford airport and suddenly being aware that I couldn't move my leg. I looked down and saw that my little brother Tyler was clinging to my leg as if his life depended on it! He began crying hysterically and begging me not to leave him. The pain I felt at that moment was almost unbearable. I felt that, like Mom, I was about to embark on a new chapter of my life, and in doing so, I was destroying the happiness of an innocent child. I remember feeling breathless with emotion and pain as I tried to gently peel the little boy off my leg. Someone—I don't remember who— held him tight as I finally walked away with my suitcases. The guilt made my heart feel like stone, and the tears just wouldn't stop. I should have been happy that I was finally getting away from all this madness, yet I was weighted down with an almost unbearable sadness that I, too, was leaving those children.

CHAPTER SIX

ᥱ

The Bond of Hope Destroyed

After leaving my children, I rarely talked about them. I simply acted as if my old self had died and disappeared without a trace. I tried to reinvent myself, and in doing so found it too unbearably painful to focus on the fact that I had actually left five beautiful young children. I began to make up facts about myself; things that may actually have been part of a dream I had for myself but knew I could never achieve. One day I told someone; "I'm working on a master's degree." Soon I was telling this to all the new people I met. Then I began to introduce myself to other people as; "a therapist working at Cooley Dickinson Hospital in Northampton." I grew my hair long and worked on being sexy and lively. My need to be noticed and liked for the person I made myself out to be was always paramount. My phony stories, the imaginary degrees and the fake job titles were a pathetic attempt to get people to think more of me than I could ever think of myself.

Normal people can cope with the issues and problems that come up in everyday life. They don't have to run away. They don't even think of running away, no matter how much pain or desperation they are feeling. They don't have to drink, and they don't experience the kind of anxiety that drives addictive behavior. In trying to run from the anxiety and the depression, the alcoholic wants to escape through drinking. The first drink might actually give some relief from the feelings of helplessness and despair. But the second, the third, and the fourth drinks are the ones that take an alcoholic down. If the first drink works, an addict assumes two might be better, and so on. The brain's pleasure center pulsates when alcohol is consumed and the addict's life is soon defined by the single-minded pursuit of that pulsation. I was addicted in every sense of the word, and my life after I left my family ultimately became a monument to alcoholism and the crazy, stupid thinking and behavior that go with it.

In Amherst, I moved in temporarily with Susan, a woman I had met in Beech Hill Hospital when we were both in recovery. In a way, the decision to live with a recovering addict made it possible for me to rationalize my departure from home. I explained it as simply "going to another recovery program." But I was choosing not to admit what was really going on. As I drove to Susan's apartment, I sensed immediately that I was going to love this part of New England and was already beginning to feel gloriously free to live as I wanted. After my arrival, Susan and I quickly fell into a routine which we thought would help our mutual recovery. For a while, we went to AA together consistently, and together we were able to stay sober.

But after living with Susan for a while, I found a place where I could do what I *really* wanted; live by myself. It was a funky one-room garage addition to a house where the toilet was placed behind a partition smack in the middle of the room. It was a hellhole of a space, but it offered me the opportunity to be truly on my own and that was very exciting. I thought for the first time in my life that I didn't have to be responsible to anyone in any way; this was a huge, selfish relief to me. I was now a full-blown, classic case of arrested development.

I got a job right away—a clue that a part of me recognized that my departure from home was permanent and that I would need to find a way to support myself. The truth was that by now I was in full flight and no longer willing to be married to Ron. My new job was that of cashier at a stationery store in Amherst. But I couldn't even make change! My inability to concentrate combined with the absence of the most rudimentary math skills threw me into a panic when I tried to process simple transactions. Because of my change-making incompetence, the lines at the checkout got longer and longer and people became impatient and cranky, even in that famously laid-back community. The manager, who at first had been beguiled into hiring me because of my appearance and glib social banter, was not amused and quickly fired me.

Next I got a job bussing tables at a restaurant where young college students gathered. But for me, all the students and young people eating there provided an opportunity to sit down with them and chat while the dirty dishes piled up on the tables and the floor needed sweeping! Socializing with the guests was not the manager's idea of what I should be doing, so he, too, fired me.

My next job was as a manager at a craft store featuring handmade pottery which was located in a little town near Amherst. But I was panicky about the money handling and basic accounting duties. Instead of seeking help or asking for a revised job description, I rationalized that I was bored with the job and soon quit. By then, I was probably only an hour or so ahead of a pink slip.

A good friend of Ron's from college, Il Koo Yun, who was a graduate student at Yale at the time, came to town to do some academic research and invited me to have lunch with him. While we talked, he sensed my aimlessness and encouraged my scattered thoughts about wanting to get a better education. I complained, "My life is going to be one short-term retail job after another if I don't finish a better degree program and find a decent career." He replied, "There's a degree program at Smith College which you should apply for. It's just right for you; the Ada Comstock Scholars program. It's for women like you whose education was interrupted. They don't care about your age." According to Smith, the women chosen to be 'Adas' were women for whom "there came a time, often years later, when they sensed an undefined and unfulfilled potential in themselves and began to wish to complete their education." It sounded like the perfect antidote to my messed-up life, but I told Il Koo Yun, "It sounds great, but I'll never be chosen. I'm not smart enough." He persisted. "Just give it a try, Jane. You may be surprised!"

I had no allusions that I was any kind of scholar. Nevertheless, I did have credits from my two-year college and at least 17 credits from the University of Hartford. I thought that maybe those credits would count and I wouldn't have to put in four entire years to get a BA degree. Lucky for me, the Ada program concentrated on a different set of admissions criteria than the normal college program. There was an institutional open-mindedness about who these women would be and what their academic records or life stories might look like. Apparently, I would not be judged by SAT scores, the number and grades of AP courses taken in high school, or a list of worthwhile extracurricular activities. Encouraged by that news, I got someone to help me write a letter to accompany the application in which I freely stated that I was an alcoholic. I also stated that I hoped the program sponsors would overlook my shortcomings and instead look for my potential. Not that I had any idea of what my potential was—I was lucky just to be staying sober! But something inside me made me want to help Smith College help me! I began to believe that maybe the college could help me become the person I was meant to be, whatever that was.

I needed a really strong letter of recommendation and Dr. Howard provided one that apparently hit the spot, because I was accepted into the Ada program. He was enthusiastic about the idea of my going back to school. He said he believed in me and thought that applying myself academically could be quite helpful to me in building a healthy life. Despite his encouragement, I had harbored no expectation that I would be accepted, and when the letter arrived, I was beside myself with excitement. Maybe I would have a future after all! Here was a priceless chance for me to achieve something that I believed could never happen. I had no idea what my future might be after earning a Smith degree, but here was the chance to find out. I was lighter than air.

When I went to Hartford for a weekend visit with the kids before officially entering Smith, Ron staged a little celebration ceremony for me, and in a sweet and loving gesture that went far beyond what I could have possibly deserved, he and the kids presented to me a Smith t-shirt as a congratulatory gift. The kids weren't accustomed to the occurrence of such a positive event in my life, and it was touching to see how supportive they were. Thus armed with their unconditional love and encouragement, I set out at the age of 38 into a sea of unknowns for which I was totally unprepared. My family then settled into a hopeless pattern of waiting for visits with me that were either disastrous or did not happen at all.

I had no idea when I started that it would take me thirteen years to finally receive a Smith BA degree. Since I had not been able to shed the curse of alcoholism before attempting this enormous academic challenge, it continued for a long time to blur my judgment and caused me to make exceedingly bad choices, to say nothing of the times when I had to be hospitalized. Over those thirteen years, I saw many Adas come and go—most of them with the coveted Smith degree in hand—and each year, I pledged to try harder to stop drinking and apply myself academically. I withdrew from the program twice and took two year-long leaves of absence. Only one of those breaks was for something positive—an internship at a Hazelden addiction treatment center which I hoped would lead me to a career of helping addicts like me.

When I started at Smith, I did not dare to face the inevitable truth; that my departure meant that I would miss all the important—along with the simplest and most banal—moments of motherhood. I would not be there for my children's first days of school, I would never again take a bunch of children to buy sneakers, or drive them to and from music lessons or soccer games, or have intimate chats with them about the events of their day, or be there to wipe away hurt or angry tears, or chaperone overnights filled with the noise of sleepless, giggling, hungry children, or see them dress up for prom dates. I would never be at school ceremonies to watch them receive awards, I would never ride shotgun next to a nervous new teenage driver, never watch an emotional teenager stomp away from the dinner table, never be there when the college acceptance letters arrived, never be there to comfort an upset or frightened child, and I would not be there when the lacrosse team won the league trophy. I would not be there for any of that. And the worst part is, I am certain my children were better off without me because of the person I was. They deserved to have a mother in their lives all the time, not a hopeless drunk who couldn't even show up consistently and whose existence made them feel embarrassed and sad.

In preparation for entering Smith, I moved out of the room with the toilet in the center. Up to the time of that move, things had been getting a bit tense where I lived because the landlord—who lived in the house with his wife—was hitting on me more overtly each day, and his wife was becoming extremely upset about my presence in their house. Needing a new place to live, I called upon Ron's help in one of the thousands of ways I imposed on him over the years, and he arranged to have me move into a recently-vacated condo he owned in the rural outskirts of Amherst. He also helped me get a job in a furniture store managed by his cousin Andy. In retrospect, I realize that Ron had asked Andy to give me a chance because I had basically become a charity case.

Apparently, Ron believed Andy would watch over me while I was working at the store, and he must have thought Andy's steadying presence in my life would help me stay sober. He was partly right about that; working at the furniture store not only gave me a way to make some money, but also a way to stay busy and sober. I began to go to AA in Northampton and was sober for the month I worked at the store. At the time, this was quite an accomplishment for me.

Andy certainly seemed like a reliable person; he had a wife and child, and made all the right sounds about helping me and looking out for my welfare. He often said reassuring things like, "I'm here to help you, Jane. We're family now. You can call on me." But Andy was hiding a big secret; he was a full-fledged cocaine addict, a problem that made him self-centered, unpredictable—even dangerous. I often overheard Andy and a similarly-addicted store employee yucking it up in the back room and had the uneasy feeling that I was the focus of some of those laughs. Andy was a repulsive man—massively overweight and pimply—and although my taste in men might have been questionable while I was drinking, I never would have dreamed—under any circumstances—of depending on a man like him for anything in my personal life, and certainly never would have considered having sex with him.

In my fourth week of working at the store, I returned to my condo after work as usual. The French couple who were renting a room from me had gone back to France for a week and I was alone. After watching TV, I went upstairs to bed. Some time later, I was awakened by the sound of the front door opening; Andy had simply let himself in because the door was unlocked. In those days, I was extremely careless about locking doors. Then he appeared in my room saying, "Hey, Jane, I was here in the neighborhood and decided to check up on you. How are you doing?" I was still groggy with sleep and was slow to catch on to what he was doing there. But then I saw that Andy had his pants down, and as he approached my bed, he croaked, "Hey, Jane, wanna see a huge erection?" Then he reached out and started tearing off my nightclothes, growling menacingly, "You want sex? This is what sex is!" I was terrified and completely helpless while struggling against his sheer physical bulk. I tried to fight back and screamed at him, "Get away! Get away!" But Andy jumped on me, covered my mouth so I could not cry out any more, and brutally raped me without another glance or a single word. When he was through, Andy pulled up his pants and abruptly left, leaving me in an exhausted, confused and defeated heap on the floor.

I was decimated by the rape, but assumed that no one would believe my story because I was a drunk and a hopeless fuck-up. In fact, I internalized the incident as being my fault. I never went back to work at the store, and it wasn't long before I was back on the booze—no job, no credibility. What the hell? I was just a drunk who didn't deserve anyone's respect. The horrible memory of that night remains vivid and traumatizing to this day, but it seems that Andy had not succeeded in forcing me to my lowest point of despair. That was still to come.

In general, during these dark years of my addiction, when I landed in bed with someone, it was usually because I was drunk and excessively needy. I was a willing participant in many such ill-advised relationships, but this incident was different—it was a brutal rape by someone who I thought was helping me by giving me a job and professing to care about my welfare. And, ironically, I was sober when it happened. Since I easily attracted men, it was easy for me to become involved with them if I chose to, and I enjoyed being able to have that amount of control in my life. I suppose it is surprising that this was the first and only time I was raped, because there were many times when I was careless and stupid while drinking and let my guard down completely.

By now I was fully immersed in a cycle of addiction in which, when bad things happened to me, I simply assumed I was the cause. After the rape, I began to drink heavily because the feelings it stirred up in me were too overwhelming to sort out or deal with rationally. And I was having a lot of trouble living with this new source of shame. To the growing list—bad mother, bad wife, bad drunk—I now automatically added the word *slut*. In my mind, all these things made me a bad person. More drinking was the means by which I sought to obliterate the feelings of humiliation and self hatred.

Soon after the Andy episode, I applied for a sales job at a successful jewelry store and turned on the charm during my interview with the manager. Once again, I got the job easily. But the man who hired me had no idea of what went on in my head and how difficult it was for me to perform even the simplest of transactions! The pinball effect in my brain along with the lasting damaging effects of my addiction—especially the inability to concentrate or perform serial tasks in any logical order—made my performance of necessary retail tasks a complete farce. My glib sociability and likeability made me effective at closing sales, but I knew that was all I could bring to the job; for me, the devil was always in the details.

Meanwhile, eager to get started on my Smith adventure, I bought my books at the Smith bookstore and began attending classes with a sense of excitement and expectation I had never felt before. I loved being a student in a serious academic environment and was in awe that this impressive academic institution was welcoming me with open arms and a promise of as much extra help as I needed. I dug into my courses with a new focus on getting the best education possible.

With my faulty reasoning, it seemed like a good decision to continue to live alone in Amherst instead of in the Smith residence set aside for the thirty Ada scholars so they could live cooperatively and provide mutual support to one another. I had convinced myself that living alone would help me study, go to classes consistently, be on time, stay sober, and go to work regularly to earn money. But that decision would soon prove to be just one more disastrous delusion. Of all the Adas in my class, I must have been the most in need of the mutual support of the others to help me stay focused and handle the challenges of Smith's tough standards. Instead, I foolishly opted to navigate alone and rudderless in a sea of temptations and self-justifications.

One day, Cole, the sexy, handsome representative of an upscale jewelry manufacturer came to the store for a sales visit and watched me fumbling hopelessly while trying to make change. That may have been one of the times when a customer mentioned with irritation that the change was incorrect, and I quickly dug in my pockets to offer her my own loose change in the hope that she would pick what she needed and I wouldn't have to struggle with the problem of making the right change.

Cole and I bantered happily in the store, and before he left he asked me out. We both felt the mutual chemistry immediately and Cole later said, "I loved watching the way you couldn't make change. In fact, I loved it so much I fell in love with you on the spot!" As for me, his good looks and fun-loving attitude produced in me a powerful sexual attraction which swept aside any shred of caution I might have possessed. Since I had just moved into Ron's condo, the only furnishings there were a lamp, a cardboard box to use as a table and some mismatched plates. Despite the sparseness of the room, Cole and I had a very sexual first night in that condo and the sounds of our intense lovemaking ricocheted around the nearly empty room far into the early hours of the morning.

I had managed to stay sober for a couple of months and certainly had not been in the market for a relationship—after all, I was still married to Ron and he was struggling at home with his demanding work life and the expanded role of sole parent for our children. But now I wanted Cole, and didn't care what it took to get and keep him. We became an item right away. One catch was that he had his own powerful addiction to pot and could not get through the day without smoking a staggering amount of it. His mother had been a severe alcoholic and had died in a fire while drunk, so Cole had experienced firsthand the ravages that addiction inflicts on a family. But, oddly, after my addiction became obvious to him, he either failed to understand the severity of my problem or just wanted to be happy in our intense relationship for as long as possible. The fact is that his enabling behavior increased my own addiction. I can only assume that my behavior did the same for his.

Now that we were totally, hopelessly involved, I completely lost my heartfelt resolve to get my world together, do well academically, get a Smith degree in a timely manner, and conquer my alcoholism. With Cole in my life, I found that I couldn't or wouldn't organize or schedule the rapidly increasing school work and instead drank in order to numb the feelings of inadequacy and pressure that were my inevitable burden in a serious college environment. And too, I realized that I had acquired a new addiction—it was Cole. I was completely obsessed with him and had no intention of trying to stop myself. The excitement of our relationship colored everything I did and every thought I had. Not surprisingly, in a breathtakingly short time, I had lost the delicate shreds of concentration and application it would take for me to scrape through even one semester of college.

At first, the fact that Cole had two young children from a former marriage seemed like a plus to me. I loved children and thought I wanted to be around his. But I quickly learned that because I had abandoned my own vulnerable children, the mere sight of his visiting children plunged me into deep feelings of guilt and despair. What do alcoholics do when they feel sad and guilty? They drink! And that's what I did—with a vengeance. There is nothing more selfish and self-involved than an alcoholic who is drinking. I was the poster child for selfish, addicted behavior.

Cole's addiction issues were of long standing. Because of them, he had gone to a high school for dropouts and had barely made it through a college—certainly not the kind of college expected by his family of Ivy League graduates. I didn't care about any of that. I thought he oozed sex and was so attracted to him that I could barely tear myself away. His expansive family seemed to like me and made a point of including me in their family traditions, but ultimately I disappointed them, just as I let down and disappointed everyone else in my life.

Sometimes people with addictions are attracted to each other because of their addictions. I think Cole saw that in our relationship. He didn't even try to stop me when I started giving up everything that had been so important to me. In a way, my relationship with him was filling up the empty hole that had always existed in my life. Although I had been trying to get my life together before I met him, the attraction I felt for him was simply stronger than anything else.

Cole lived in Greenfield—a little town only 20 miles from Smith—and introduced me to a little community of people he thought I could fit in easily with. Of course I could; they were all potheads and cocaine addicts! I was pouring down the vodka non-stop at that point, so who was I to object to their lifestyle? There has always been that badass part of me, and these people with their drug addictions and problems seemed very exciting.

Although I was not staying sober, and was not following through at Smith, the mere fact that I was a student at a prestigious college gave me an identity I never thought I could have. I was proud of telling people that I was an 'Ada' because everyone in that area of New England knew what that meant. But I certainly wasn't earning the proud title of Ada; no, I was regularly skipping classes and hopping into my car before the weekend even began in order to escape to Cole's place. I just couldn't wait to get started on our time together. To drown the guilt about skipping classes and getting behind in my school work, I started drinking as soon as I got into the car—at first it was the inevitable two bottles of wine that I carried in a book bag stowed in my car. As our relationship continued, it was two bottles of vodka that I always kept in the seat beside me. Like a cartoon character in a strip that could be called *The Worst Person in the World*, I swigged right from the bottle and when it was empty, casually threw it out and listened happily as it smashed into a million pieces on the road behind me.

During one of my desperate escapes into the arms of my pot-addicted beloved, I was so drunk by the time I arrived in Greenfield that I was driving on the wrong side of the road and was quickly arrested. At my request, the police called Cole and he came to rescue me at the police station. They knew him—his family was prominent in that community—and took him at his word that I did not usually do things like that. God knows how many near accidents I had while driving back and forth between Northampton, Greenfield, Hartford and Amherst while drunk beyond comprehension. Yes, Hartford belongs on the list too; I was driving my own children back and forth for visits while drunk and getting drunker.

If I thought some of my scenes with Ron early in our marriage were worthy of the alcoholic degradation seen in *Days of Wine and Roses*, the addicted, alcoholic weekends I spent with Cole were exponentially worse. He started every day with pot, and as the day wore on he added increasing amounts of alcohol to the mix. I was always drunk, and because he was with me, he was drinking heavily too. When Monday came around after these addiction-fueled weekends, I often bagged going to my classes at Smith in favor of staying in his apartment and drinking his vodka while he went off to work in a cloud of pot smoke. When I drank most of his vodka, I replaced what I drank with water—a favorite trick of alcoholics. I was like a little chemist, mixing my phony potions—in this case water with the remaining vodka—to hide the painful and ugly truth; that I had consumed everything alcoholic within my reach. When I had consumed and watered-down too much of his supply, I pulled myself together enough to drag myself into town to buy replacement vodka.

I was drunk in the mornings now and driving drunk every time I was behind the wheel. All my dreams of earning a Smith degree and finding a profession had gone south with dizzying speed and were lost in an alcoholic haze. My new friends in the Ada Comstock program worried about me. When I finally reappeared briefly on campus they asked frequently, "Where were you?" Other times they said with alternating concern and reproach, "I missed you in class." My AA friends started calling me regularly and asking about my absence from meetings, but I still stubbornly refused to accept an AA sponsor and there was no way of influencing me or controlling my behavior. I didn't want anyone's advice, and apparently I didn't care about the concern my friends and fellow addicts were showing. And so, after only one semester, I was hopelessly behind in my college work and concentrating only on my messed-up addicted relationship with Cole. I had completely lost my way.

This is where things get really fuzzy. When an alcoholic makes the claim that the fine details of his or her drinking life are still vivid enough to write about completely accurately, it's a lie. We are drunk when most of the important things happen in our lives and we can't remember details clearly. Or, we have blackouts and can't remember anything at all. Here's another ugly fact; after a while, our excessive drinking causes generalized memory loss— or, more bluntly, brain damage. So I am not going to claim that I have a firm grip on the details of my trip into alcoholic hell which escalated while I was addicted to Cole. One thing I know for sure; it wasn't pretty.

Oddly enough, there is one thing I do remember throughout that whole period. Even with all the drinking and serial failures, I never lost the feeling in my core being that I was going to finish Smith and become a winner instead of the chronic loser I was proving myself to be. Even in the depths of my drinking, when I couldn't even focus on something in front of my face, I still felt that I had embarked on something life-changing—the Ada Comstock Scholars Program at Smith College. At some corner of my brain I had stored the notion that this was a challenge I would find a way to finish. I would make something of myself. The problem was, I had this little problem with alcohol...

Drinking trumped my college dream just as it had trumped family life with Ron and my five children. When I realized that I couldn't hide that ugly fact, I went to the dean and got a medical leave of absence and left the program without committing to a return date. The college administrators were very understanding about their Adas; presumably, I was not the first alcoholic they had seen in the program.

Soon after leaving the Smith program, I began the seemingly endless cycle of rotating in and out of rehab. By that summer I was afraid of the savagery of my addiction and decided to go to Hazelden to get help. When I told this to Cole, he said, "Why are you going to Hazelden? You aren't that bad!" Such was our mutual state of denial. But by the time I entered the twentieth treatment center, I had become a little less arrogant about what I was capable of doing without professional help. Still, despite giving a little more of myself to each new program I entered in the hope of being cured, I remained hopelessly addicted.

Cole finally broke up with me when I arrived at his place for Thanksgiving a little over year after the beginning of our intense and screwed-up relationship. We were supposed to be spending the holiday with his family, but I arrived very late and walked into his place drunk. He took one look at me and said, "You are late, you are drunk, and this is my family we are going to see. Jane, I just can't deal with your drinking any more." I was fond of his dad, and Cole's whole family had embraced me until I started to go over to the dark side more and more and was drunk whenever they saw me. This last time, I was a disgusting, staggering mess. Oddly enough, Cole was the first person who had ever openly condemned me for that behavior; but he himself was a hopeless addict in his own right! I was stunned at the hypocrisy of it all, but simply said, "Okay," and got back in my car and drove away.

Somehow I was able to drive from Cole's place back to my condo in Amherst without having an accident and then drank away the rest of the holiday. Now I had a terrific excuse for drinking. I was medicating the loss of my boyfriend—my obsession—with massive amounts of alcohol to the point where I couldn't feel anything at all. And I quickly found another guy to fill the empty place. There was always another man in the wings who wanted to be with me until I hurt him so much he couldn't take it any more. Men wanted to fix me and they all thought there must be a magic key to achieving that. They just didn't understand that I had to fix myself, and I was not even close to doing that.

After my breakup with Cole, and my failure at Smith, my new boyfriend dumped me on New Year's Eve when we had plans to go out. He was supposed to pick me up at my house, but it was late and he still had not shown up, so I called him. He said, "Jane, I don't want to see you any more, I have moved on." When we hung up, I was so devastated that I began chugging alcohol. I drank so much I eventually passed out, fell against the brick edge of the fireplace and smashed my nose. When I opened my eyes, blood was everywhere, and I was lying in a pool of partially dried blood. Thousands of black flecks in my vision made seeing clearly almost impossible. I have no idea how long I had been lying there in my own blood—perhaps a day or two, but who knows? It could have been longer than that.

As I lay there unable to see properly or move in any purposeful way, I waited for death to come. I thought, *So here it is. This is the end of my life.* It was an oddly comforting thought. Finally, my struggles would be over. The images of my children appeared to me. I thought of them standing with Ron and a new wife on a playing field on a cold January morning. The picture seemed okay to me. They had their home—the Ronald Household. They all had friends and family; people to wipe away their tears.

I remembered that one of my girls had said to me once, "Tyler wishes that you were dead." I was comforted that my passing would finally make him a happy person. I thought of the pain he had endured because of me. I saw the painful image of him waiting outside the house for a mother who couldn't stop drinking long enough to be with her son. It was too much for a small child to bear. I cried out, "Oh God, let this be over." This time, I meant these words.

Eventually, at some point during those quiet hours, I began to feel differently. That little light inside me began to glow again. I began to lose the idea of dying. And I was finally thinking clearly enough to drag myself across the floor to where the phone rested on a counter. I couldn't raise my head, but grabbed the cord and pulled it until the phone clattered noisily to the floor. I couldn't see the dial clearly, but somehow I managed to dial 911.

An ambulance came quickly and the attendant was very kind, talking soothingly to me as he strapped me onto a gurney, wheeled me to the ambulance, and sat with me while the ambulance proceeded to the hospital. Once there, he stayed with me and talked to me about recovery. He told me his own story—said he was a recovering alcoholic—and mentioned that he could see that I was an alcoholic and he wanted to help a fellow addict. His words were kind and understanding, and he seemed like the only person left in the world who would waste his time on such a ruined person as me.

The medical staff told me I had suffered a bad concussion and my nose had been severely broken in the fall. Days later, when I was able to leave the hospital, I still had blurred vision, a pounding headache that was to stay with me for many weeks, and was sporting two enormous shiners to offset the huge white bandage keeping my ruined nose in place.

Soon I was in yet another rehabilitation center and at the beginning of another of a long series of attempts to climb out of my miserable state. At home in Hartford, Ron was beginning to understand that I was gone for good. I knew I had broken his heart and handed him a whole new set of problems, and the truth is, no matter what he did for me, or how much he cared about me, I was not at all willing to work on staying with him. Nevertheless, he was always hopeful, and at the end of my rehab stay, while he and the kids were vacationing in Nantucket, he invited me to join them for a vacation. I suppose he thought I might change my mind and try harder to come back to my family if I spent some time with them in that relaxed seaside environment.

We had gone to Nantucket before as a family and I associated the place with family bonding. But since I had lived on my own for a time, I was reasonably sure that I would never choose to go back with Ron. Consequently, it was a very painful few days, and I ended up leaving early. Ron's deal from the beginning was that he wanted us to be sleeping together at night like a married couple. I suppose he believed that reestablishing our former intimacy would somehow heal the fractured relationship. But while he tried to overcome the problems of the past with intimacy, I lay there rigid, with tears streaming down my face, realizing that I hated being with him. This was a moment of truth for me. Finally, I sat at breakfast in tears and said to the kids, "I'm so sorry, I can't do this any more." Ron later drove me to the ferry.

My departure from Nantucket that day signaled the end of the marriage and the end of my motherhood for a very long time.

Kris

My stomach churns as I come to understand how selfish and self-centered my mother was in those days when alcohol was more important to her than her kids. Her pretending to be a single person, or even a competent person with a graduate degree, is beyond my comprehension. Imagine what it feels like to learn your mother pretended you didn't even exist! Imagine learning that your mother—who used to be present in your life—chose a life of debauchery over life with you. Thank God we didn't have to deal with this drunken woman on a daily basis. All my mother's bad decisions were likely to bite her in the ass and they did.

I'm angry that Pop covered for her every time she screwed up. I understand that he loved her but he put the younger kids' lives in jeopardy on so many occasions by trusting her with their safety. Her drunk driving could have killed them all.

Hallie: When I think of how Mommy was driving those young kids around while she was drunk, I am shocked. We still ask Pop how he could have let that happen. She had a way of pulling herself together to trick him into thinking she was not too drunk. She had a way of pulling herself up straight to look in control but Kris and I always knew what that meant. That, and the bloodshot eyes gave her away to us.

Lindsey: I always noticed that Mom's drink of choice was vodka and orange or grapefruit juice. When she had a glass of something, I always took a sip of it when I was with her to see if there was booze in it. The three of us younger kids went to visit her wherever she lived in Amherst or in later in Farmington, and we often rode in cars with her while she was drinking or drunk. I have confronted our father about this many times. His answer has always been, "Lindsey, what was I going to do?" I think it was more important to him for us to have a relationship with her and to love her.

Ron: I will readily admit that one of the biggest mistakes of my life was allowing Jane to drive our children around while she was drunk. I did not realize until some people started telling me that Jane was doing this. It was stupid of me. My driving and Jane's driving are two different things. In my generation, we drove when we were drinking or had been drinking. I'm not bragging about it; it was a fact of life. But Jane should not have been behind the wheel of a car. The dumbest thing I have ever done is to allow Jane to drive down from Amherst to pick up the kids and drive them back. Our kids had friends and wanted them to go to Amherst too, but their parents knew what was going on and didn't allow them to go. One of the mothers told me, "I just don't trust Jane with my child." That was when I woke up to the full extent of the problem. The truth is, by then I had seen Jane passed out drunk many times, and why I did not think of the driving problem, I do not know. It was just stupidity on my part.

I remember begging Pop to cut off the money so Mom would learn how to fend for herself or die in the process. Unlike Pop, I often didn't care whether she lived or died. Doesn't that sound so cold? Well, she disgusted me so much that eventually I really didn't care. She was right in thinking the younger kids were better without her. It makes me cry thinking about them wanting their mom, unaware at an early age that she was so sick and maybe even hopeful she would come around. But Hallie and I knew better.

We all needed our mom, yet there she was living a different life and pretending we had never been born. It's sad because my mom was so nurturing when Hallie and I were young. She nursed all her babies and showed us love, but then alcohol got in the way and slowly she turned into someone else—a stranger. She is very fortunate she was married to Pop, because I cannot imagine many men putting up with the stuff he tolerated. But in this dark phase of her alcoholism, it seems her charm could only get her so far; and even that was slowly fading.

Let's go back to the day my mom left for good; so much for our happy family summer vacation. People dream of going to Nantucket and we were blessed to be able to go for the entire month of August. My mother hadn't been there to help pack us up for our vacation or get us settled into our little vacation rental home. She just showed up from somewhere else after we had settled into a comfortable, relaxed vacation routine. I nervously watched her talking to Pop; she seemed stiff and uncomfortable. I couldn't read Pop's mood. I was desperate to figure out what was going on between them. I'm not sure if the younger kids sensed trouble; but I certainly did.

Now my parents' situation becomes cruelly apparent; Pop is yelling, "You'll have to tell the children yourself!" For once he is refusing to do her dirty work for her; no more excuses from him to keep us close to her. She is on the spot for this one. Now we are all gathered together in the kitchen to hear her say, "I can no longer do this."

I know she is talking about being with our family. She can't do this anymore? Do what? What has she been doing? Pop tells her to keep explaining. She blurts out "I don't love your father any more and I am going to leave." So it's true! Now we know what we have always suspected. It's not just Pop she has stopped loving. Surely she means us too. She doesn't love any of us! She just wants to leave us. Just like that; she's leaving us forever.

Suddenly I am lost in a deep dark place, not knowing what to say or whether I can even look at my mother. Pop sees our faces and starts to try to hold things together, to make it better for us the way he always does. Soon Mom is grabbing her things and then she goes to the car. Just the three of us are in the car now, driving down to the ferry. I am watching Pop's face. It says it all. Mom gets out of the car and I don't even give her a hug good-bye. I am too numb. We watch her walk to the ferry, and at some point, Pop gets back in the car and crumbles like a small child.

Pop cried so hard after Mom disappeared onto the ferry, he couldn't get control of himself. Pop—our family rock—was falling apart before my eyes. It hurt me so to see him in this kind of pain. Fear, hurt, anger; who knows what was welling up inside him? As we drove back to the house, I reached over to help him steer the car, afraid we would have an accident because Pop couldn't even concentrate or see through his tears.

Now that I was so worried about Pop, I didn't have time to examine my own feelings about what had just taken place. I'm not sure I ever let myself cry about her departure. In a way, it was nothing new.

What did my mom feel? Did she feel anything at all? Who had she become? Was there anything left of the person who had loved us and was supposed to be our mom? Pop and I tried to move on before we even got back to the kids; we had kind of a tacit agreement to pretend we were having a good time from then on. I guess we thought that would help the younger kids.

After that day, I felt a greater responsibility for my siblings. Pop never asked me to take on these responsibilities; it was what I wanted—perhaps needed is a better word. But then the recurring dreams started disturbing my sleep at night. They were terrifying dreams of helplessness when I tried but failed to protect my siblings over and over. These dreams are still vivid in my mind to this day. There was a cliff in the dreams—maybe it was the cliff where Pop lived with some friends before he married Mom; where he and Mom had their wedding reception and where his drunken friends grabbed the couple and threw them into the lake like stones. I remember myself as a child looking out over the edge of that cliff and feeling my stomach harden in fear.

Time and time again in those dreams, I see the youngest kids in their little pajamas. I am taking care of them but walk away from them briefly. Suddenly a line of soldiers appears out of nowhere. The soldiers are in full gear and create a human wall around the kids. I can only see the children through the soldiers' legs. They are wild-eyed with fear and looking for me to rescue them. I hear them calling out for me to help them and I run toward them as fast as I can. But the soldiers are pushing them back, one step at a time, closer and closer to that cliff. I start reaching for them but can't seem to grab onto anything. I can see their big brown terrified eyes as the soldiers start pushing them over the cliff. I lunge forward to catch them but they are gone!

Suddenly I am awake, not sure if I have been awake or dreaming, and my pillow is soaked with sweat and tears. This dream tormented me for months and months and I knew I was in a bad place emotionally. But I was too afraid to mention my own state of mind to anyone. Above all, I didn't want Pop to worry about me, so I stuffed all my feelings deep down inside where I thought they would be safe from probing.

Hallie was terribly affected by mom's drinking and her absence from our lives. Like Mom, my sister always made friends easily. Although she had quite a temper on her, I believe it was anger about Mom that started to come out during her teen years and it changed her. I remember her slamming some girl up against a locker in high school because the girl had done something to a friend of hers. Hallie badly needed a mom to give her the kind of loving support only a mom can give. As Mom's substitute, I was just too busy with the young kids and couldn't give Hallie what she needed. Besides, she didn't seem to want me in the mother role. We were too close in age for that. I just wish someone had been there for her.

Hallie: Mommy had been away, but we thought she would be coming back to us soon. We were all in Nantucket and she was back with us, but they were sitting at the kitchen table and she was saying she didn't love Pop. He made her say that in front of all us kids. I think he was doing this to punish her because he was so hurt. It seemed to me that he loved her more than any man could love a woman. He was bawling when she repeated these words to us, "I do not love Pop."

... I think I fought with Kris about taking over the mother role when our mother left for good. I wasn't comfortable that she was in charge and I think I acted out worse than if she hadn't been. Maybe some of the resentment occurred because Pop spoiled her because she took over the mother role and that was helpful to him. She never got in trouble, and Pop always gave her credit cards to do what she wanted with. On the other hand, I was always in trouble and resented Kris.

Our biological dad should have paid better attention to what was happening to Hallie, but he was too lost in his own relationships. When he was not dating someone, we saw him fairly often, but while he was dating a new woman, there were long periods when he just wasn't present in our lives. Pop was trying to keep things together at work and at home; I doubt he had much time to give to Hallie, except he did enjoy going to her soccer games. Thank goodness Hallie had such a great group of friends because they kept her on an even keel most of the time. I envied those friendships because I couldn't open up to my friends the way she did. She was an open book, spoke her mind, and was always testing the water. On the other hand, I was too afraid of my own shadow and was too embarrassed by what was going on at home to open that door with any of my friends.

Pop and Mom traveled a lot before I was able to babysit, and they would leave us with Mrs. Sullivan—let's call her Sergeant Sullivan! She was a strict sitter and took any frustration she had out on Hallie. Poor Hallie, she was always getting in trouble with Mrs. Sullivan. No wonder my sister resented me so much. Things generally ran smoothly when Mom and Pop were gone, but I lived in my own little world of books and my imagination and I don't remember getting into trouble. But I didn't talk back or cause trouble. Hallie tried to run away once and Pop didn't try to stop her. She made it to her friend's house and I think was gone until after dinner.

God help any person who crossed Hallie during her teen years! Thankfully she had soccer; it helped her work out a lot of her anger. She was and still is a fantastic soccer player who was never afraid to attack. Pop loved her fighting spirit and was very proud of her successes on the field. Mom seemed oblivious to all of Hallie's successes. Today, Hallie's boys are well behaved, polite, energetic kids who know they are well loved. A positive thing that came out of Hallie's upbringing was that she has always been clear that she doesn't want her children to feel the way she did while growing up. Without going overboard, she shows them how much she cares about them. Hallie has always shown my children a lot of love and has always been there for me when things were difficult in my life. As we matured and began to talk about things, our relationship began to flourish and grow. Mom missed out on so much. It is sad that she can't go back through time and correct some of the damage. Every memory we created as siblings, she missed. Those memories just don't exist for her.

I should mention some of my mother's choices in men after her marriage with Pop. How did my mom manage to find these guys? I guess *they were probably the only ones who could put up with her drinking since they were mostly drinkers and potheads themselves. In the days when she had her act together, heads always turned when she walked into a room and finding someone to date was probably never an issue. But keeping someone in her life even for a short time was a different story. We kids met all types of men she was hanging out with, and to our eyes, she didn't seem to belong with any of them.*

The younger kids spent more time with the men in my mother's life than I did because I was on my own for much of the time when she was stringing along a rogue's gallery of men. I'm guessing that some of these guys didn't even know that Mom had five children. And I think they certainly couldn't have imagined that she left us to search for whatever it was she was trying to find as she sang that stupid song about how it's her time! I think her reaction to that song was only getting her closer to death.

Courtney: Most of my childhood memories of my mom were when she was no longer living with us. However, I do have one memory from when she was still with us, before she left. I was really young at the time. I remember my mom and dad standing in the kitchen talking one night. Mom was drinking some juice—something that they used to argue about—and I took a sip of it. It tasted awful—like poison. I knew then that she was drinking something she wasn't supposed to drink—and it was the thing she and Dad used to fight about. I remember Mom taking the glass away from me abruptly after I took a sip. She seemed angry and sad. I remember going upstairs and sitting on top of the staircase that led to the kitchen, listening to Mom and Dad argue, and feeling sad. Then I went to my room and cried myself to sleep. I had been hoping my mom would come up and talk to me about what had just happened but she never did. That is my only memory of her living at home with us.

Lindsey: The fact that she left might have been our

mother's greatest gift to us. When she was gone, we no longer had to deal with her on a day-to-day basis. One thing about Mom, whether she is drunk or sober, she just leaves when she is not comfortable. She just tunes out and leaves. It's a self-protection thing.

As to Mom's boyfriends, I met Cole but I didn't care to know him or any of the others. I knew my mom had strong feelings for Cole and realistically, he may have been the only one she ever cared about. He was tall and handsome, but I cannot remember much more than that. It's important to understand that when you are a kid thrust into visiting your mom and she brings a man around to meet you, the men are more like blobs to you than people. I didn't care about them—who they were or what they did for a living. They probably looked at me and thought what a strange girl I was, but I wasn't willing to pretend they were anything more than just another guy in the revolving door of my mom's life.

Mom's work history was a joke! Everyone wanted to hire her—even when she wasn't qualified— because she had the charm to win over most potential employers. How many times did I hear her say, "I have the best job; they love me and I am making so much money," only to find that she stopped showing up or got fired because she didn't know what she was doing? These jobs were fantastic only for the days or the week she was able to hold them. She was very lucky that Pop still supported her. Also, her parents kept sending her money and she had a trust fund from her grandfather! She could pretend all day long that she was a real working person. I guess she was trying to impress us kids and make herself feel better, but bottom line, she didn't really have to work.

It used to make me angry when she talked about how tough it was for her financially. She didn't know squat about how hard it is to survive financially; she lived in a dream world and no one was willing to burst her bubble. People continued to pick up the pieces for anything that went wrong in her life. For most of us, when a job isn't going well, we have to suck it up and fix the problems because losing a job is not an option. Mom just didn't have to take work life that seriously. I am not trying to take away from the pain she must have felt when she wasn't numb with alcohol. And I know that her life was sad and desperate because of her alcohol addiction. Today, now that she is well, we can all listen to her stories about those jobs and laugh at her pitiful attempt to hold one down, but back then, it all simply disgusted me.

My mom's Smith years are very blurry to me. I knew she liked going to college and made some nice friends there over the years. Of course they all liked her! In Jane's world, "everyone loved me!" I was happy to see she was trying to do something with her life, but at this point, I was slowly losing interest in what she was doing with and to herself. For a long time, I was building such a strong sense of resentment towards her that I dreamed of how much simpler life would be without her in it. I often got upset with Pop and told him to stop protecting her all the time – to let her survive on her own. Pop often told me that the younger kids still needed to be able to see their mom. He didn't want them to have memories of a poor drunk woman living at some halfway house. He never let Mom fall on her face financially or when she was in trouble in other ways. Once again, he and other people were picking up the pieces for her. Pop told me he thought about letting her suffer on her own, but just couldn't do it.

Tyler: Unlike all of my siblings, I have no memory of living with my mother. It's not that my mother was ever foreign to me, but all of my earliest memories are of a time when my parents had already split—in living together, but not necessarily divorced. I'm told that the memories I do have—a trip to Disney, a family vacation in Nantucket, etc. were all during times when my dad was trying to salvage the relationship and include my mother in family events. I also have memories of arguments between the two of them, with my mom storming away in the end.

I adored my mother through those early years. Everyone seemed to have so much love and adoration for her. Even though she was clearly doing so much that was wrong, to me she could do no wrong. It was always heart-breaking for me to hear that we had to cancel a visit. More often than not I would be sitting around the living room, or looking out the window, with a bag packed for a trip to mom's house. I remember very deep feelings of pain and disappointment. At some point, and while I was still at a pretty young age, the reasons for my mother's absence, as communicated by my dad or older sisters, went from her being sick to her being drunk or in a hospital. I started to understand that no visit was guaranteed.

I have three distinct memories that marked the distance I was trying to create from my mother. The first was when she showed up one time to pick me up for a visit. She walked around the front of our house, to where I was playing in the front yard; I saw that she had chopped off her hair. She was no longer the long-haired beauty that I'd been enamored with. She was somehow ugly to me.

The second memory was of my mother surprising me at school (I was in 2nd or 3rd grade). She showed up in the school cafeteria to have lunch with me. However, this was after she'd had a major accident that resulted in a broken nose and blackened eyes (I believe she passed out from drinking and smashed her nose). She was not only ugly to me, but I was mortified by her very presence. I hated that I felt embarrassment about my mother.

The third memory was of a time when my dad said my mom had gone missing—they didn't know where she was. This dragged out for a couple of days. They ended up finding her in some drunken condition, but she was alive. I remember wishing that she was dead.

Ron: In our living room of the last house Jane and I bought together is a large painting of the five children; it was painted in the fall of the early '80's when Jane was living in Amherst and on her roller-coaster. A picture/painting's worth a thousand words. The four girls are standing and sitting around one of the large white columns on the porch as a group and Tyler sits to their left, kind of alone; isolated.

For whatever reason, this picture stands out in my mind as a remembrance of the day when Tyler (about the age of 5 or 6) was sitting on one of the steps on the walkway, by himself, with his small suitcase by his side, waiting for his mother to pick him up. My recollection is that they were first going to the amusement park—Riverside Park in Massachusetts—and then to Jane's condo for the weekend. I might add that previous to this time the mothers of the kids' friends had stopped allowing their kids to join Lindsey, Courtney or Tyler in Massachusetts for the weekend because they all knew of Jane's drinking exploits and rightfully were trying to protect their kids from any possible incident. In the past Jane had made a collection of promises to all the kids and each disappointment was like a punch to the stomach for me. Yet at the same time, I would always try to protect Jane and make excuses for these actions—not necessarily a cover-up, but excuses.

While I was honest with the family about their mom's alcoholism, I loved Jane and was probably too protective. I mention the many disappointments for the kids from their mom—specifically, the lack of communication for weeks at a time. I remember Jane showing up with two black eyes, shattered nose, different men, etc., etc. Yes, I was angry, embarrassed for the kids and probably madder than hell as I took the kids' pain so very personally. Bottom line, each disappointment was an attack on the family and me.

Anyway, about the day the picture reminds me of: Tyler was dressed to go, with baggage in hand and was excited about his date with his mom. He wanted to wait outside to be ready when she drove up. Even with all the prior disappointments, his love for her continued. Yes, Mom was late—no cell phones to communicate with her—and I'm sure I continued to make excuses as to where she was. And he continued to wait outside. But finally the little boy was crying with anger and disappointment. He was a wounded animal with only his father to protect him. His sisters were not on the step then to divert his attention. Finally he came back into the house and went alone to his room.

He was alone then as he is in the painting in my living room and while I cannot reflect on his words and emotions, I can say I felt the hurt and the anger in my soul. Mrs. Prebble—our surrogate mother, sitter, cook, and family inspiration who came to us after Jane had left for good—had said many times to me, "Some day the hurt and disappointment will be so much that the 'bond of hope' of Jane coming back to the family will be broken." The hurt to me that day was the straw that destroyed that bond of hope for the family ever getting reunited. Jane was sick. Jane was selfish. Jane was not with us. Jane was not coming back and I would never again allow her to hurt the family as she did Tyler that day.

CHAPTER SEVEN

୭

Mrs. Prebble to the Rescue

After I left my family for good, Kris held things together at home as surrogate mom, and then a 300-pound savior named Mrs. Prebble came to the house each day and did the cooking and the driving for the children and saw to it that the household ran smoothly. Just as I had Rosie in my life as a child, my children had Mrs. Prebble. She was an enormous, gospel-loving white woman from the other side of the tracks who had her own family to look after as well as ours. She became an indispensable person in Ron's household from this time forward. I came to think of her as a saint.

Unfortunately, Mrs. Prebble's arrival was hardest on Tyler because he loved me dearly the way a small child loves his mother and had no possible way of understanding why I had left him. He was a sensitive and emotional child and cried often and inconsolably, making Ron impatient and fearful that he was not displaying enough manly characteristics. In fact, Ron was eventually to send Tyler to a psychiatrist, an experience that did little to allay the little boy's very understandable uncertainties and fears inflicted by his mother's final departure.

Mrs. Prebble's old car was an embarrassment to the kids. The exhaust was noisy and smelly and the car was full of paper wrappers and old food. Kris remembers begging Ron to not make them go anywhere in that embarrassing car! But despite her car and her overall appearance, Mrs. Prebble was able to win over the kids almost immediately and got them to laugh again after the trauma of seeing me leave for good. She also got them to hold hands and say grace together at meals. These were things they badly needed to keep them together as a close unit. She used to say, "Pray for your mother, pray for your father, God help us all." She helped them with homework when they were in elementary school. And she helped them with any number of problems that children go through. Courtney and Lindsey consider her their guardian angel. They have told me, "Mrs. Prebble is still looking down on us." She came every day and understood how vitally important she was to our damaged family.

After my breakup with Cole and my exit from the Ada Comstock program at Smith, things had taken a very dark turn and my life became a series of unhealthy relationships with men fueled by prodigious amounts of alcohol. I dimly remember many incidents in which I was driving drunk and throwing my empty bottles out of the car. Several emergency hospitalizations followed— I can't remember how many—and my overall memory of events becomes even more elusive as I try to reach in and grab at fleeting snippets of truth. The closer I get to the darkest side of my story, the fuzzier my memory grows.

I was kidding myself, but I moved from Amherst to an apartment in Farmington—a town that was close to Hartford—with the idea that I would be able to see more of my children. My mother, despite her usual state of denial about my addiction, had pushed the idea, thinking that being closer to the children might possibly help me get sober. Surprisingly, she had become a more positive figure in their lives than I could have ever hoped for. She and Ron still did not care for one another, but nevertheless she had taken on a role of provider of material goods and grandmotherly indulgences to my children. I consider it nothing short of a miracle, but they loved her unreservedly, did not feel her controlling power and were untouched by any of the behaviors that caused me so much sorrow and anxiety.

My move to Farmington had only one advantage that I could see; I would at least be closer to my family during my emergencies and inevitable death. And the kids did try hard to reconnect with me. But our relationship always felt forced and it was very clear to me that I was a mother in name only. After all, I was but a visitor in their world. I feel certain that my children did not enjoy having me closer to home because I was in terrible shape. The proximity and more frequent contact seemed to mean only that they were often the unhappy witnesses to my further descent into oblivion and felt increasingly powerless against its gravitational pull. When I was with them, I often could not wait until I could be alone again with a bottle of vodka. Even when I was with them, I affected great cheeriness on the surface, but only if I had some booze in my body. Thinking I was hiding the booze, I carried around an ever-present McDonald's cup half full of vodka and half with diet Coke. Outwardly, my attitude said, "Hey kids, here's your fun-loving, happy mom!" Inwardly, I was barely holding on until I could be alone again with my bottle.

Realizing that my move closer to the children had made my relationship with them worse, not better, I allowed a man to move in with me. Greg had been living with his sister, but found the prospect of moving in rent-free with me and having bedroom privileges was far more exciting. I had long ago left behind any real interest in sex other than for the opportunity it gave me to exert control over men. They would fall hopelessly into my power and all I had to do to get it was climb into bed with them. Greg was a classic enabler and bought me alcohol whenever I wanted it, while also rescuing me by taking me to rehab when I needed it. Ultimately, I moved to another condo, and Greg moved back in with his sister. Without him to watch me, I began a precipitous slide into a very, very dark period. I was getting sloppier and more unkempt by the day. I bruised easily and became uncharacteristically uncoordinated. I went to Reid Treatment Center for detox ten or more times, and Dempsey Hospital three times. I went to Blue Ridge Hospital two times and then to the Hartford Hospital psych ward three times. In each of these instances, when I was discharged to go home, there was no aftercare plan to help me maintain sobriety or even a semblance of a normal life.

As my drinking progressed even further, so did the decline of my physical and mental health. There were numerous times when, after a week of heavy drinking, I had run out of alcohol. I knew the stores opened at 9 AM, so I often tried to drive to a liquor store for my morning fix. But I was starting to have severe anxiety attacks while driving and would often have to pull over to the side of the road to take deep breaths while clutching the steering wheel. My legs were rubbery, and my hands were trembling so badly that I couldn't get out the correct change for the early morning pint. I began to notice the store clerks' expressions—a mix of curiosity, disgust and pity—and I had a very hard time making eye contact. I was a just hopeless drunk now, trying with my last droplets of energy to appear normal.

Once back in the car, I would frantically open the screw top on my precious friend, lift the bottle to my lips and gratefully—oh so gratefully—gulp down the biting warmth of the vodka. This would bring immediate relaxation and I could then drive back to my place where I could spend the morning watching TV and drinking until I passed out. When I awoke, I began the insanity all over again.

I occasionally went cold turkey in anticipation of a visit from one of my children or an old friend. In my mind, cold turkey was definitely preferable to detox, but when attempting it, I was always afraid of having a seizure when there was no booze in my system. To avoid submitting to temptation and to calm myself down, I would walk around the block—a short walk—but by the end of the walk, my face would be flushed and I would be sweating profusely. I tried going to AA, but while there, I worried that others would notice that I had been drinking heavily. It would be very hard to miss the glassy eyes, flushed face and smell of vodka seeping from my every pore. And of course, there was the ever-present shame which I must have telegraphed with my apologetic body language and facial expression.

But at some point, I reached a point beyond shame. I just didn't give a shit any more about hiding anything or pretending to be someone else. The idea of getting and staying sober seemed completely beyond my power. How could I get there? I thought;

If I ever do get there, will I be one of those 12-steppers I saw at AA meetings—those smug, self-satisfied winners? Would I have to make new friends? I couldn't trust myself, so how could I ever trust a friend?

I was an equal opportunity drunk. Somewhere along the way, I lost track of how many one-night stands and affairs I had. Friends-with-benefits was an arrangement that came easily to me. I only cared about the conquest of a man, not in keeping him. How fucked-up is that? I lured into my web every possible sort of man—from a Yale-educated architect to a *bona fide* cowboy, to an insurance executive, to an authentic down-and-out street person. One of my conquests was a handsome doctor who was attracted to me until, on our fourth date, he came to pick me up for dinner and I greeted him in full cry; tottering around, glassy-eyed and slurring my words. He was cool and said, "Why don't I leave now and then call you later about dinner?" Lucky guy, he never called. During this dark time in my downhill slide, Ron finally made the decision to divorce me. I was in no shape to battle him in court for money, property or child custody. Nevertheless, I did retain a lawyer who took on my case because he knew Ron had a lot of money and could see that I badly needed a source of consistent support. Ron's lawyer was a big-name guy, so our divorce began as a David and Goliath kind of thing. But when my lawyer suddenly died in midst of our divorce negotiations, Ron got his lawyer's associate to take my case! Despite such an outlandish conflict of interest, I overlooked the inequity because of my overwhelming guilt and shame and readily signed away my rights to my five children and to the house in which I had a substantial investment. I was left with a set income each month and what was left of the trust fund from Grandfather Stevens that could not be broken. It was a good thing I had those sources of income because I was in no shape to earn my own living.

Ron is a sympathetic character in our harrowing story. He was not a good husband and father until I left and then he was forced to step up and become more involved. He stepped up because he is an honorable person, and in the process, he became a better father. Today, all these years later, the house where Ron and

I lived on West Hill is filled with pictures of all those wonderful moments that families share. It is pathetic that among the hundreds of photos displayed on the tabletops and on walls, my face appears only once—in that long-ago photo of Ron and me at our wedding. It looks like many other photos of young brides and grooms, except that while I was posing demurely with a glass of champagne in my trembling hand, I was puffy-faced and glassy-eyed with a major hangover—not beset by bridal jitters as a stranger might logically assume.

Among all those joyous family photos, I am not one of the faces behind ski goggles and grinning in front of a mountain backdrop, my arms around a couple of kids. I am not waving to the camera from a chaise lounge beside a pool filled with laughing, wet children. I am not bent over watching lovingly while a small child blows out candles on a birthday cake. I am not the bath-robed figure passing out presents on Christmas morning. I am not behind the camera either. Instead, I am the unseen ghost haunting my family's past, present and future. I am the apparition challenging my children's future happiness with the constant reminder of what their lives could have been without the taint of their mother's crippling, all-consuming addiction.

Ron eventually married the woman he had been dating. Jean was unhappily not able to have children of her own and was eager to plunge in immediately and be a mother to mine. She did so enthusiastically, and it seemed, with the confidence of a seasoned mother, firing Mrs. Prebble in the process and pushing the teen-aged Kris aside in order to take over the care of the younger children herself.

Despite his new marriage and our divorced status, Ron continued to show up in the myriad emergency rooms where I ended up in severe alcoholic distress. He was sincere in his desire for me to have a relationship with the children and was willing to endure Jean's unhappiness about these visits and his obvious continuing emotional connection to me.

After the divorce and Ron's subsequent remarriage, there were many uncomfortable moments when I showed up unexpectedly at a soccer or lacrosse game and tried to talk to Ron alone. At times like this, his new wife invariably tried to insert herself between us and nudge me out of the way. Apparently, at some point I began to hint to her falsely that Ron and I were still sexually involved and then cruelly delivered body blows to her in the form of malicious personal comments like, "You'll never be anybody's mother." Understandably, these alcohol-tinged attacks caused an enormous problem between Jean and Ron, and eventually sucked a bloodthirsty Eulalia into the fray. Hostile letters were exchanged and Ron's characteristic tolerance of my many sins was finally shattered. It is telling that I don't even remember what my manipulative behavior might have been that brought him to the end of his rope.

> **Letter to Me from Ron:** *This is not a hard letter for me to write. The anger and disappointment within me concerning your verbal accusations to Jean last week is very shocking to me and indicative of a sick mind. Further, your attempts both to destroy my marriage to Jean and to draw the two older girls into your allegations of the existence of an ongoing affair (after my marriage) have finally made me put an end to any communication with you at all.*
>
> *Jean and I chose to ignore the several occasions in the past when you have accused me, again to the two older girls, of an ongoing sexual involvement with you. But now you have taken the unforgivable and totally vicious step of approaching Jean directly with your barrage of lies. Indeed you seem to have made a clean sweep of this, having included your mother in your delusion. This can only be further evidence of your total lack of caring for the children, in fact for anyone but yourself.*
>
> *...Your cruelty to my wife has gone beyond even my tolerance... You have to be accountable for your actions. I am certain you can find someone to sympathize with your current situation but you alone know the truth of what you have done. In the final analysis you have to live with yourself and all that you have done. ... I would hope that from this day forward you will reclaim the esteemed name of Bartels and let my name stand only within this family...*

Letter from Ron to My Mother: Over the years your history has shown your character to be that of a very controlling, selfish and demanding person who insists on having life only one way... your way! Tragically you have never learned to let go of attempting to control your children and thus Jane, as the doctors would say, still functions at the level of a grown teenage child... especially when it comes to accepting responsibility for her own actions. She is being held accountable by us for her fabrications in this matter and you are being held responsible for viciously passing this information on to my wife and others. Jane's love/hate relationship with you (usually at her convenience) is accentuated by your constant interference and sadly this has contributed additionally to her demise.

We are no longer interested in your accusations regarding our singular or collective influence on Jane's drinking and/or her mental health. Your direct accusation to my wife that she is responsible for Jane's current/past/future drinking is nothing short of ludicrous. Jane has been on her own road to self destruction for the last 15 years that I have known her and tragically even before that.

While I was living in Farmington, I tried to work, but found that I couldn't hold a job because of my unpredictable behavior, state of mind and lack of sobriety. I always had a guy in my back pocket, and was always saturated with booze. Most of my mornings began with a throbbing headache, dry mouth and a single-minded desire for more of the poison that had put me in this sorry state.

My morning ritual begins as I drag myself out of a sweat-soaked bed—the bile from last night's binge bubbling up in my throat—and head directly to the kitchen counter where my second bottle of vodka awaits; the first bottle having been emptied during last night's binge. The days of simply *wanting* a drink are far behind; now I *need* to drink just to start the day. Standing over the sink, I carefully pour a shot into a glass with a little orange juice and toss it back quickly. Swallowing this first shot is followed by several moments of dry heaving. The gagging finally over, I pour the second shot. Down it goes until a warm glow settles in and gives me blessed relief and steadier hands. I am starting to feel better—almost comfortable, in fact. No more danger of heaving into the sink; now I can turn on the TV and spread out on the sofa with a full glass of vodka and orange juice. Flushed with well-being, I am the center of a new happy family; the vodka and the chattering strangers on TV. I tell myself I feel comfy and protected now; but really, all I feel is numb.

In these dark days, some of the men who ask me out are healthy, and when they realize what a mess I am in, bow out of the relationship quickly. But the men with addictions or psychological hang-ups stick around and happily party with me until they cannot continue to watch me destroy myself. I suppose it is a blessing that much of this period remains indistinct in my memory. Nevertheless, a few indelible memories do remain—at least from the early days before I lost the ability to leave the couch and could not work or even look for work. Some of those memories are amusing in a kind of grotesque way.

I get a job at a Chevrolet dealership and sell cars like a madwoman because people find me entertaining and willingly give me the sales out of friendliness. I even manage to sell a dump truck to one customer. But I have no idea how to do the paperwork involved; each time I make a sale I have to flirt suggestively with another salesman or a manager to get them to do the paperwork for me. Despite some success and a lot of help from the men who help me with those annoying details, I eventually lose the job because I am drinking heavily and not showing up for work.

Soon I get another job. This time, I am watering plants in office buildings. To a normal person, this might seem like a less-than-challenging activity, but for a person like me with a screwed-up mental compass it is almost impossible. I know nothing about plants! But as usual, there is a man in charge of the hiring, and he is captivated by my bullshit and what is left of my good looks. He doesn't even ask me what I know about plants or watering and he has no clue that I have no sense of direction. My brain just can't work through the concept of North, South, left or right. Office complexes can be confusing to me when I am sober, but when I am drinking and impaired, the situation becomes hopeless. Often I become completely lost, wandering aimlessly in hallways until someone shows up and points the way. When finally I get to the right offices, I can't figure out an orderly system for watering. One day I walk into an executive's office to water his plants and sit down to chat with him. I never get around to tending his plants.

I am supposed to be pruning and dusting the plants as part of my duties, but instead I am chopping off living branches without any clue as to proper pruning methods. I have been trained for all of this, but can't retain any of that information. Training me is like trying to train a very young puppy with selective hearing; I just can't engage well with people telling me what to do. I am hired for my personality and clients enjoy having me around, but eventually my failure to show up, combined with the total absence of competence, comes to haunt me and I am eventually fired from every job.

I simply cannot stay sober. As the intake and frequency of my drinking increases, I begin to experience panic attacks and paranoia. I live to drink. But in truth, I am essentially drinking to tolerate living. Ultimately, I end up in the detox unit at Dempsey Hospital where my father visits me just before the *delirium tremens* kick in and then goes home to write my obituary.

Dr. Howard ultimately tries putting me in the Institute of Living, a psychiatric hospital. No one knows what to do with me, and this is his way of trying something new in the hope that it might somehow break the cycle of addiction. But putting me in a mental ward is not a good idea. It adds a whole new form of trauma to my already confused existence. I am terrified every moment of my first stay at the place because my roommate frequently suffers psychotic episodes and chases me around our room with a broom trying to kill me. Nothing personal, I guess. She simply confuses me with the devil, or whatever demonic vision fills her with dread.

The third time I go to Beech Hill I begin flirting with a counselor named John, who is a big 6'5" Harvard-educated guy. He is a recovering alcoholic who works in the detox unit. I have become adept at flirting with any attractive men involved in alcohol programs because it helps pass the time. After I move to the rehab program, John and I begin sleeping together in a cot set up in his staff dorm room. By the time I am released, our relationship has taken on a more sinister aspect as he has become obsessed with me. John drives to my place one night while very drunk, breaks down my locked front door and waits, sitting in a chair in my living room, until I return. There is no alcohol in my place because I am staying sober. But John is sweating, shaking uncontrollably and demanding, "Go get me some booze. I need it NOW. Go!" I am terrified that he will try to kill me.

It seems that no one has ever been in as many detox units as I have. In fact, I was a kind of self-appointed detox guru. Like a restaurant critic, I could have written a guidebook of all the good and bad aspects of each place I stayed in. *Detox Units I Have Known* would contain my expert ratings of drying-out places. I told myself, *I could do a better job of running this place! I could be a better counselor than so-and-so is!* Group meetings, free time, counseling sessions, all the fucking homework assignments—it all became one big hackneyed blur. I believed I could bullshit my way through anything and fool any counselor. Underlying all of this was my certain knowledge that when I left the place, I would once again be gloriously free to drink.

I was totally self-centered and narcissistic. But somewhere beneath this unattractive, self-absorbed surface, I was a shame-based woman who hated herself. Nevertheless, a small flicker of light in that dark soul kept me going. Some might call this the presence of God. Some might call it a remnant of a younger Jane—"the person everyone wants to be." Whatever the small flicker was, it ultimately—miraculously—became a beacon of hope in my otherwise bleak, grey world.

All detox facilities, whether public or private, are highly democratic places. Although there are vast differences in the quality of the food and the beds, they are alike in the way the clients are treated. A person could be a CEO of a major corporation brought to the facility in a BMW or he could be an unemployable homeless person wheeled into the place in a grocery cart by a down-

and-out friend, and no one would recognize or care about the status differences between the two men. I made friends with everyone—including the staff members. These were the people who often greeted me warmly during my multiple returns to their care. I still recall one day when I reappeared at one detox. A young male staffer briefly lost his look of professional detachment and said to me sadly, "Oh Jane, what can we possibly do for you this time?" Then I just gave him that apologetic embarrassed laugh I had developed for such occasions.

The places I cycled in and out of form a crazy quilt of memories now. As I became a repeat visitor in too many of these places, I learned the names of staff members and they always greeted me with reassuring hugs and compassionate glances. I don't think they ever got used to having such a young, hopeless charge as I was. When I arrived I was always in horrible shape; often so drunk I was barely aware of my surroundings although I think I was always able to muster the fake-happy greeting and a self-deprecating laugh at the situation. Once a staff member mistakenly thought I was alert enough to find my own bed. She pointed down the hall and said, "Third door on your left, Honey. Just find a bed on your own and I'll be with you soon." I dutifully followed her instructions, but didn't realize until many hours later that I had climbed into a cot with someone else—a nameless, grizzled old drunk I had never seen before.

Recovery always felt 'good' because I was away from my usual messed-up life. It gave me structure, people to bond with, and physical healing. It was a relief to be able to walk the outdoor pathways between the assigned group therapies. In those days, there was never any suggestion of "aftercare planning" and this was a serious problem for someone like me. The lack of support each time I reentered my regular life was an instant threat to my fragile sobriety. I might come home and immediately enter in to AA meetings with great enthusiasm, but after a while, the escape into drinking was the more powerful urge.

Because I lived alone, I was a target for men seeking vulnerable women at AA meetings. I remember one man who drove me home from a meeting and asked if he could spend the night at my place. He was insistent and belligerent when I told him to leave. I later found out he had made a bet with some other men in the meeting that he could get me into bed that night. For some men, this kind of thing is called "13th stepping". In other words, they focus on the meat market aspect of AA and use it to cruise for available women. For me, AA was not always the safety net it is intended to be. This is hardly surprising, considering the fact that a roomful of recovering addicts is a room filled with unwell people who are capable of many things. Dangerous and co-dependent relationships can be formed there because of the extreme vulnerability of lonely and lost people.

At Spofford Hall, where I went for several 28-day programs, I joined in a circle each night after dinner and sang *Amazing Grace* with gusto. In the Greenfield detox—where I was taken many, many times—we drunks padded around the ward in our paper slippers and formed a merry band which found humor in grotesque things. A group of us laughed uproariously at one drunk who had smashed his false teeth, put the broken plates back into his mouth in the wrong places and glued them in with Super Glue. We were still laughing when he was carted off to an emergency ward to have the mess removed.

The Springfield detox was a cement structure, damp and dark like many other facilities of its kind. Thin curtains divided us from one another and we learned of each other's unseen presence from the chorus of unbelievably loud farts, belches and demented shouting and groaning that formed a constant drunken symphony. At Reid Treatment Center, where I went over twenty times for detox, I knew the nursing and kitchen staffs by name. They always greeted me warmly upon my regular returns. At Dempsey Hospital, I was a patient at least three times in order to undergo detox by an intravenous method.

At the Hartford Hospital, I was placed in the psych ward and a concerned friend left an unexpected gift for me at the front desk. It was a pair of fuzzy pink bunny slippers. What an odd picture I must have made padding about in these iconic symbols of childhood innocence! While in this ward, I was assigned to a psychologist who was a Freud-like character with a full beard and an ever-present pipe which he constantly fiddled with and chewed on. While I poured out my sad stories to him, he routinely fell asleep. This proved to me beyond a doubt that I couldn't even keep a paid psychiatrist interested in such a pathetic life. My sense of self worth was so low that nothing surprised me.

Eventually, I decided to leave Farmington and move back to the condo in Amherst. I owned it now as it was given to me in my divorce settlement with Ron. I knew I needed to live cheaply because I was going through my inherited money quickly. If I hadn't received money from my grandfather's estate, I probably would have been homeless. When I think of that, I am acutely aware that I could have ended up like my grandfather Bartels— dead on the streets from alcoholism, then disposed of by the Salvation Army because his disgusted son was unwilling to claim his body.

Kris

We called her Ma Prebble. She came into our lives at a bad time for us all and she showed us what some structure could do for a messed-up family. She was a huge woman, but she put me on a diet when I was in high school. Pop had told her to do it. He used to preach to us about taking care of ourselves and watching our weight. He criticized women who were heavy and yet he took on the biggest one of all to put some order into our lives and keep my weight under control!

Ma Prebble drove this big, ugly car that was messy and cluttered, belched blue smoke and always seemed to be on the verge of exploding. Every week, she piled the three youngest kids into it and took them to the store with her to buy our groceries. What a funny image that made; three little bodies sitting helplessly in the back seat, while being driven by this enormous woman wearing a ridiculous-looking turban on her head.

Ma Prebble boiled low-cal chicken and vegetables to feed me according to a strict diet and then sat at the kitchen table herself—legs spread apart to give her stomach room—and ate waffles with ice cream as a snack! At the time, I was 5'9 and weighed 145 lbs—150 on a bad day. Not so big! Ma Prebble's non-diet dinners were awesome; and she always had us sit together at meals and say a prayer. This was something new for us. Although we may have balked at first about the changes she introduced, we ultimately found them very comforting. She seemed to know how to handle most situations and was very sweet to us. Eventually, I came to love her; but from a distance. I wasn't about to let anyone get too close to me at that time. We all have fond memories of her.

Courtney: I remember the day Mrs. Prebble came into our lives. She came over to the house to meet us all and she seemed very intimidating to me because she was very large, and old-looking. Not like my young, thin, and beautiful mom. I was told that Mrs. Prebble was going to watch over us every day while my dad was at work. This made me feel sad at first, but in time, Mrs. Prebble let me help her in the kitchen, and I looked forward to the times when she brought her little dogs to our house for us to play with. Mrs. Prebble let me sit on her lap and she sang songs to me—songs which I sing to my own son today. Mrs. Prebble made me feel loved every day, and for this I feel forever grateful. To some extent maybe her love helped me from going down a different road.

My dad was my other saving grace—the main one. Although he worked every day, he made a point of coming home in time for dinner as often as he could so we could have a family dinner and talk about how the day went. Dad supported us in every way. He was at all our sports events, cheering us on and videotaping us. He even tried to help coach our teams when he could. He made every holiday a special occasion—taking us to the haunted house on Halloween, taking us on weekend skiing trips, to the ocean in the summer, and Christmas shopping in NY or Boston, or at G. Fox and Co., in Hartford. He came to tuck us in bed if we wanted him to and he even took the time to kiss all my stuffed animals goodnight (well, some of them at least). My dad was a rock star of a father. He was not perfect—but his heart was always in it, and he made me feel loved and special, even calling me "Special Courtney".

Lindsey: All my friends' parents were divorced. But I was the only one of them being raised by my father, while they were with their mothers. It was kind of awkward. Mrs. Prebble was a wonderful person to have taking care of us because she adored us. She was religious, and the thing I liked about her 300 pounds was that she could embrace us and completely envelop us with her body. She had to keep us in line, but her idea of discipline was making us sit in a "thinking" chair for five minutes. Once in a while, more serious infractions brought benign taps with a wooden spoon. She was always there when Mom was living away from us and made a date to come and pick us up but never showed up. I remember this happened pretty often. Sometimes when she did show up, it would have been better if she hadn't.

My fondest memory of Mrs. Prebble happened in my senior year of high school. Today it still touches me deeply.

All the senior girls were required to wear white dresses for graduation. I am not even sure who bought mine for me. It should have been Mom, although it most definitely was not. All my friends' moms were present for their daughters; they helped them choose dresses for the graduation ceremony and the senior prom that evening. But I had to fend for myself. I didn't have a dress for the prom. There just wasn't anyone around who thought of helping me get one. But as the day approached, Ma Prebble was upset that I didn't have a prom dress and thought about how much I needed my mom. She thought about the problem and told me she would solve it. Then she bought ribbon and little flowers and sewed them onto my graduation dress to make me feel special. I remember noticing her rosy cheeks as she presented her handiwork to me. She had tried her best to fill the void left by Mom. It was one of the priceless moments in my life.

Courtney's graduation—nine years after mine—confirms how important Mrs. Prebble was to us, and also reveals Courtney's ever-present hope that somehow Mom would change.

Courtney: When I look back at my high school graduation in 1993, I remember feeling that I should be excited, but what I really felt was nervous and anxious because I had invited my mom to attend. Everyone was going to be there, but was Mom? She had told me she would be coming but she rarely kept her promises. I figured she wouldn't show, so I didn't allow myself to get my hopes up. Then the thought went racing through my head; *What if she shows up drunk?*

I knew how tough it was for Mom to be at any function my dad and my stepmother would be attending together. My stomach was churning due to not knowing what this day would bring. I thought; *I shouldn't have to worry about this stuff! It's my graduation day!* This was so me... always worrying about someone else—mainly Mom! Then I thought; *Where will mom sit if she comes?* Families were arriving early to get a good seat and Mrs. Prebble was there for me—as she always was.

Just when I am thinking Mom isn't going to be there, she shows up AND she appears to be sober! Thankfully, Mrs. Prebble has saved a seat for Mom, which makes me relax and begin to enjoy my day. But then my thoughts start to wander... I'm thinking; *It's good to have Mom here but she doesn't even know who I am!* What a huge sense of disconnect. Here is this woman watching me graduate from high school and she doesn't know anything about my experiences in school or any of my friends. *Ok, she is here now,* I tell myself, *but she has missed so much of my life.* Most of the families sitting around her are hugging and celebrating, remembering their kids' accomplishments, yet she has no memories of what I have achieved. Finally I stop stressing and tell myself; *Just be happy she's here!*

I have a picture of Mom from that day. It is still framed and on display. It's one of the few pictures I have of her taken before her recovery. To me, it is proof that she was trying to follow through on her promises. She was trying to make up for so many promises broken. She was trying, but at the time I really doubted that it would last.

Ron: When Jane was living in Amherst and later in Farmington, she would show up with a black eye or something, and a couple of times I couldn't reach her and drove to Amherst and found her passed out at the bottom of her steps. I used to worry and often called the Amherst police. In 1982, I got involved with Jean [who I later married], but I was still holding out for Jane. It was Mrs. Prebble who told me that I would never get Jane back. She said, "Ron, she won't come back. She's a sick person." It wasn't until I went to Alanon one time because of Jane that I heard the horrible stories of what happens to women alcoholics. I felt bad for them. It was there that I learned that I could not change the situation. That was the first time I heard about the concept of "hitting bottom." I realized then that I couldn't do anything for Jane. I knew it was her battle. And I decided to let her go.

I wish I could say I had warm feelings for Pop's second wife Jean. But I am not going to lie about the relationship. Jean began dating Pop when I was still in high school. I think it was at some point during my junior year—or was it my senior year? I have a great memory, but if something isn't important to me, I often don't register it in the memory bank, so this date is simply not there. Jean was well-manicured and a stickler for manners. I didn't like her, so I avoided her at all cost. Pop and I had been doing just fine until she walked into the picture. I know she was sizing me up just as I was checking her out.

The younger kids seemed to be more interested in having Jean around and I completely understand that they needed someone to be their mother. Since she couldn't have children of her own, a single dad raising five children must have been a perfect opportunity for her! She could step in and be a hero. I couldn't warm up to her then and to this day, I still don't know if I understand her. But while Jean and I struggled to get along, it is important to understand that the younger kids needed her and she provided necessary structure in their lives. They undoubtedly have a very different take on what she brought to the table, and I know they are grateful that she was in their lives. Jean made all of us accountable to her, and this was something very new to me. I had lived a good part of my life without anyone questioning me and now I had to answer to another woman? It was inevitable that I would have a problem with her moving in and taking charge of our household.

I guess I understand why Pop sent those letters to Mom and Grandma. These were some of Mom's dark days, and she was doing all sorts of ridiculous things. I know that Mom always tried to convey to us the idea that Jean was the bad person in our lives. As part of that, she tried to get Hallie and me to take her side when she made false state-

ments about Pop. She told us he was continually trying to get her to have sex even after he was with Jean. At the time, I was disgusted that Pop would bribe my mom for sex; but in fact, that never happened. No wonder Jean was so cold to my mom! There was a jealousy between the two women and I think they envied each other for different reasons. I thought at the time: *to hell with both of them!* I once mentioned to Pop how much I hated Jean and he held up a stool as though he was going to throw it at me. Of course he didn't throw it, but I can see why he was so upset. Based on all the limited information I was dealing with, I had come to the conclusion that she was not a good addition to our family. Was it because I felt slighted? Maybe. I constantly worried; *Will the kids still come to me for help and love? Will they still feel the same about me?*

Jean wasn't warm like my mom could be when she wasn't drunk. Oh, how it bugged her when Pop's mom mistakenly called her Jane, as she did for many years. Even Pop often transposed their names and that angered her even more. I secretly found this very funny. But despite all my conflicted feelings, I knew that Mom was in such a bad place that our lives were much easier without her.

While this book is not about Jean, she has her place in our story. She was a good addition for the younger children; I just didn't want any part of that. To this day, they have maintained their own relationships with her despite her divorce from Pop. I know Mom was envious of Jean and the way she managed to make her way into the center of our family life. Even before she married Pop, Jean was included in our trips. And the family photos which decorated our house after Pop's marriage to her included Jean while there were no such pictures of Mom. Our mother was being pushed further and further away from us.

None of us wanted to be with Mom because it was too wrenching for us, but the sad fact was that we yearned for her and still loved her. There were times when we became hopeful during those short bouts when she said she wanted to quit drinking, but those times were few and short-lived. In the long run, we stopped trusting that she was capable of ever telling the truth. Lindsey, as the middle child, saw more of Mom's worst period than I did and has her own version of the nightmare our family endured.

Lindsey: When you come from a family of five kids, siblings are often the bane of your existence, but when you are children of an alcoholic mother, they are your lifeline. As a child, I became increasingly more protective of my younger siblings. We were the ones who spent overnights with our mother, and as the youngest three of five, Lindsey-Courtney-Tyler became as one word. Perhaps this was because my older siblings had grown tired of mom's alcohol abuse, incessant lies, and manipulation, or perhaps they just had many high school obligations that took up their time. In any case, it was often Courtney-Tyler-Lindsey who visited mom in Amherst. Being the oldest of the three, I developed some wisdom about my mom's abuse that I still don't understand to this day.

The three of us were a team, and I was the Captain. I was the one in charge, while Courtney and Tyler mastered the art of defending and I guess you could say I was the offense. I was the one who proactively sought out mom's vodka-infused cocktails and hidden empty vodka bottles. I was the one who awoke to her midnight trips to the kitchen in search of more alcohol. I was the one crying myself to sleep knowing that my mom thought we were so naïve we wouldn't notice what was going on. I guess at various times we were all protectors of another sibling. We were like dominoes in our interdependence. Because I was the oldest of the younger kids, I developed the drunk radar and took it upon myself to protect them. Unlike me, Courtney was Mom's staunch supporter. Anytime I addressed mom's drinking, it was Courtney who was quick to defend her by saying, "Mom can't help it...she has a sickness."

Like my younger siblings, I remember Amherst for many reasons. Most vivid were our many (compulsory) trips to Dairy Mart. These trips were not compulsory because we *wanted* to take mom's money, walk for a mile by ourselves and cross a very busy street to buy a Blow

Pop. No, Mom mandated these visits by telling us to "Go and get out of the house...here is some money, get out and go to Dairy Mart." Her tone varied by visit and according to her level of desperation. Sometimes it was enthusiastic, while at other times it was agitated and urgent. Either way, I knew exactly why we were told to get out of the house. Even at that young age, I was wise enough to know that she needed thirty minutes to drink. In thirty minutes she could drink a lot.

Like all of my siblings, I remember mom's short temper, bloated appearance, broken nose, and infinite number of missed visits. But unlike my older siblings, we younger ones had a lot of overnight visits with Mom during some of her darkest periods. In spite of these periods, there were some great times, like trips to Sweeties candy store and to Northampton for homemade ice cream. Staying the night, 90 minutes from the comfort of our home, resulted in a plethora of emotions: Anxiety, Euphoria (from the few times she was sober), Disappointment, Sadness and Doubt created a chaos of emotion. I was anxious about her ability (or inability) to drive a car, euphoric in the presence of her sobriety, disappointed in finding that her orange juice did, in fact, have vodka in it despite her claim otherwise, but mainly I felt great sadness for her, sadness for all of the irony. There was irony that she looked like hell when she could have looked beautiful, irony that a mother of five was always alone, and irony that she was 'liberated' from the family and yet was a captive to her own alcoholism. Like every other addict, Mom's life revolved around the bottle and all the familiar norms of motherhood went out the door.

A mother-child relationship is like no other. Children look to their mother for support, guidance, affection and love. In the absence of that, they have to seek it elsewhere. I sought it from my father, our caretaker Mrs. Prebble, and my siblings. Our biggest fear was not how this disease would affect us but how it would affect Mom; that it would kill her. Was she going to die on our watch? Would she get into a car accident and die a gruesome death? Would she be alone when she died? If she died, we would be forced to live without her forever. While my siblings might have felt otherwise, I never wanted her to die. I just wanted her to be sober in the way we had seen after her many rehab stints. I wanted her to look like she had so many years ago. Seeing my mom in a string of treatment facilities made me sad, and leaving her there left me heartbroken.

Courtney: All of my other childhood memories of my mother came from very sporadic visits with her. My earliest memories are more pleasant than not, although they were sad and I often felt lonely. She moved to the Amherst area of Western Massachusetts. I usually went up with my brother Tyler and sister Lindsey. Mom usually came to West Hartford to pick us up, although sometimes my dad would drive us there, an hour away. My mom tried to make our visits as pleasant as possible, making us a cozy bedroom, offering us overstuffed sandwiches for lunch, and making my favorite dinner—chicken or pork chops with seasoned salt, lemon and butter. To this day I don't know if she knew how to cook any other dish, but this was my favorite nonetheless and I looked forward to it every time. Mom always rented us videos or took us to a movie, which we enjoyed. My favorite part of the visits came when we went on 'Moon walks.' She had little ponds near her place, and we would go for walks when it got dark, looking for the moon and listening to the frogs croak. It was a very peaceful and fun adventure for a kid. Although we usually enjoyed our visits, we knew when she was drinking because she would be acting weird—distant— and would send us kids on a long walk by ourselves to Dairy Mart to buy candy. Sometimes I would just search around her house looking for hidden vodka bottles—which I always found. I knew I would find what I was looking for and it was always a sad find for me. I guess it was kind of a sad game I played just to see how many I could find, and where. Mom also had a variety of boyfriends. Some of these we liked, but others we didn't. Some we really, really didn't like.

I never really knew when I would see my mom. Many times we had plans for visits with her and she didn't show up. My dad would have to give us the news that we wouldn't be seeing her this time after all. Sometimes she sent us cards—but she was known for never writing anything other than, "I miss you, Love, Mom." Nevertheless, it felt good to receive them. Many times Mom wasn't available for visits because she was away in one treatment center or another. When she moved from Amherst to Farmington, and my sister and I were teenagers, we were able to visit her there on our own because we could drive. But often that was pretty awful. I remember one time when I wanted to visit her but my sister Lindsey and my brother Tyler refused to come with me because they were angry at her. I argued with them that drinking wasn't her fault, that she had a disease. But in my heart I didn't even believe the disease excuse. I felt that drinking was a choice, but nevertheless, I felt so sorry for her being there all alone that I wanted to try and be there for her. I went by myself and it was so sad, like all the other visits. She looked like crap—her hair a mess, wearing sweatpants, and her eyes glossy and glazed. She just looked so sad—like a caged animal going through the motions in a place she was forced to stay in. On visits like this, I always cried as I left. It was heartbreaking.

I came to a realization some time in my teenage years that my mother would not survive. She had been struggling with alcoholism for so many years, but she just seemed to get worse and worse. I was always on edge waiting for the phone call telling us our mother died. I truly believed that as I got older and had a family, my mother would be only a memory. I thought she would not get to see what I had become because she tragically let herself slip away. In my mind, no matter how much love and support we tried to give her, she would not take it and instead chose death over life.

I may be wrong about this, but I think that having loved Mom with all his heart must have made it very difficult for Pop to open up and give his affection to any other woman. Understandably, this must have been very hard for Jean. Pop eventually stopped mourning the loss of his marriage to Mom and moved on with his life, but the five of us children must have been a constant reminder of what he had with Mom before alcohol ruined everything.

CHAPTER EIGHT

☙

Christmas Memories

The annual Christmas party at our house when I was young was usually a rare happy time for our family. My mother—always transformed into a nicer mother briefly for the holidays—always made a huge pot of vegetable soup for our Christmas Eve dinner after which we all went to church where my brothers sang in the choir. It seemed to me that my family was emotionally connected and bonded at those times—and only then.

When I was married to Ron, my happy childhood feelings about the holiday were replaced by alcohol-numbed residual memories and I was usually very drunk while wrapping packages and getting things ready for the kids' Christmas morning. New traditions arose. For instance, because I always greeted Christmas morning in the throes of a gigantic hangover, I conveniently instituted the practice of serving champagne at breakfast and claimed it was in celebration of the holiday. In truth, I needed it to stop the shakes.

Christmas Day, 1980. The drinking on Christmas Eve continues with the Christmas Day visit to my parents' house for the traditional family party. On top of the bottle of champagne I consumed in the morning, I toss down bloody Marys and other mixed drinks for most of the day. Sometimes I have to sneak the booze because Eulalia has embarked on a not-so-subtle conspiracy with the other party-goers to keep me from drinking. Does she think she's fooling me—a professional drunk—when she hands out mixed drinks to everyone but me under the lame guise of a festive non-alcoholic punch? She has not taken any serious steps to hide the booze supply and I know where to find what I want. During the day, I eagerly pour what I need into my virgin punch. I can beat her in any game she decides to play.

Christmas Day, 1983. It is now well known to everyone that I have been cycling in and out of a large number of treatment centers. My parents decide to lock the liquor closet before my arrival to keep me sober. But I find a way into that locked treasure trove by picking the lock. Christmas has always been all about drinking in our family; no one can take that cozy memory away from me, however hard they try.

CRX Christmas crèche. I am driving in my little Honda CRX while in near-blackout mode. The car is on autopilot and suddenly hops the curb in a Farmington neighborhood, headed straight for a nativity scene that is lovingly arranged on someone's front lawn. While I watch passively, the CRX—with me in it—runs over Jesus, then Mary and then Joseph. Only barely conscious, I have managed to flatten and crush the Holy Family on a stranger's lawn; the broken faces are now embedded in the ground and various limbs are spread about the yard. Slowed only slightly by the remnants of these hapless victims, my little car keeps going, seemingly lured by the brightly lit Santa that waves to us like a jolly host at the foot of the front steps of the house. Within seconds, Santa meets the same violent demise as the Holy Family. Finally, the car comes to an abrupt stop, unable to climb more than halfway up the steps. The owner of the house—whose presence I finally notice when he begins pounding on the windshield of my car—is not at all amused. He tells his wife to call the Farmington police while he stands guard over me. He needn't have bothered; I am incapable of going anywhere.

According to the police report of the carnage that night, I bit one of the police officers when he tried to interview me. He then arrested me and hauled me off to jail. Combativeness like this was not my style—I was usually a cooperative and happy drunk—but I have absolutely no alternative memory with which to refute his claim. Later, someone came—probably Ron—and bailed me out of jail so I could go home. When I later appeared in court, I was required to pay full restitution for the neighbors' destroyed Jesus, Joseph, Mary and Santa as well as a whole new lawn. Although I was surprised about the biting part, I always owned up to my bad stuff, even if I could not remember it. And so, when my crimes were laid out in court, I cheerfully stipulated to my destruction of this homeowner's cherished holiday tableau and accepted the punishment.

Christmas lockout, 1984. After her marriage to Ron, Jean quickly becomes fed up with the problems I have brought into her life while she is raising my five children and running the household I abandoned. She finally takes the situation in hand when I arrive laden with Christmas presents for the kids. She meets me at the door and says coldly, "Just leave the presents outside, Jane. You don't need to come in." Shocked, I passively do as she requests and then reluctantly but obediently drive away. This is a first for me. I am not only unwelcome in what I still think of as my house, but I am not allowed to see my kids. I can't fault her, but after this unaccustomed reaction, Christmas takes on a whole, sad new meaning for me. I begin to dread what had once been a happy time and try to obliterate it with a more mind-boggling intake of alcohol than ever before.

Christmas in the psych ward. I have been seeing a psychiatrist in Amherst who becomes convinced I have multiple personality disorder. She wants to help me get in touch with my other "selves." Her therapy sessions involve coming to my place, shooting me up with some sort of 'truth serum', and observing me as I babble my version of the truth. I tell Dr. Howard about this curious practice and he investigates and reports her for breaking professional ethics rules; she never practices psychiatry again.

After dispensing with the truth psychiatrist, Dr. Howard sees what terrible shape I am in and sends me for the second or third time to the Institute of Living where I am assigned to the psych ward. This place is a real shocker—patients shuffle around aimlessly in their own troubled worlds, often talking and gesticulating to whatever specters exist in their imagination. Being zoned out from a mental disability seems to me akin to being zoned out on booze but with an important difference. A drunk can sober up; a mental patient needs medication to even begin to approach normalcy. The new doctor decides that I am bipolar and that heavy doses of Lithium are the solution. In my sorry state, I think that having a bipolar diagnosis is somehow better than being just a drunk. So I gladly take the meds. I tell my family happily that the problem of my drinking is solved. "Yay, I'm bipolar! All is well; we finally have a diagnosis." All are relieved. A happy ending is in sight—right over there where the rainbow ends with a pot of gold.

On Christmas Day at the Institute, I find myself marching zombie-like around a fir tree on the Institute property, holding hands with a bunch of nutty patients zonked out on powerful drugs. We sing Christmas carols in a strange, dirge-like tempo until the nurses determine it is too cold to continue the outdoor part of our not-so-jolly celebration. Despite my drug-induced fog, I still know that alcohol is an important part of who I am. I think; *Will I ever be able to part with it? Who would I be without it?*

Eulalia's last Christmas season 1987. My mother has had a stroke, and after a period of time during which her condition is determined to be hopeless, my father makes the decision to have all machinery and tubes removed so she can die. It is December— her favorite time of year.

With my life in a shambles and crashing down around me, I sit alone in the room holding her cool, unresponsive hand and watching the monitors recording her rapid disintegration. Outside in the hall, I hear a familiar Christmas carol coming from a speaker and a nurse humming along with Bing Crosby. As I sit at her bedside, I find myself intently focusing on what is left of my powerful, intimidating mother and uttering a prayer-like exhortation in a voice I barely recognize—a voice from deep within my soul. It cries out to her unconscious body by repeating over and over; *Give me your strength! Give me that strength that so controlled me! Give it to me so that I may find the strength to beat my addiction!*

Eulalia dies soon after this interlude and a wave of overwhelming relief rushes over me, pushing aside some of the flat-line numbness that I have come to know so well.

Christmas Season, 1991. I am back in Amherst trying to piece together a pathetic life with another loser, Bill, divorced father of two, sometime carpenter and druggie black sheep from a wealthy family. I met him while we were briefly paired up to sell insurance door-to-door in Connecticut. Needless to say, neither of us was suited to that kind of work—I couldn't even begin to master the paperwork and he couldn't sell—and we drifted into a sick, addicted relationship in which we were pursuing a half-assed plan to buy and restore an old farmhouse in Amherst.

Bill is a type of loser I know well—the only kind of man who ever chooses to stay with me after discovering the depths of my alcoholism and my unending power to disappoint and hurt those close to me. On this day, he is angry and hostile because I have begun once again to attend AA in a desperate attempt to save my life and crawl out of addiction. Any attempt to get myself together is a threat to him.

I am upset after a disastrous visit from Courtney during which my drinking was obvious to her and she revealed that Tyler refused to come. In response to Bill's shouted questions and his paranoid accusations, I finally say, "Get the hell out! Don't come back! I don't need this from you!" In response, he picks up our fully decorated Christmas tree and hurls it across the room and then walks over and smashes it to pieces against the wall. As he stamps out the door and out of my life forever, he screams out his final Christmas blessing to me —"Fuck you!"

As I pick up each piece of shattered glass and shred of tinsel, I view the mess as a metaphor for the past 20 years of my life—shattered dreams and shredded lives. The mess seems like a large puzzle with many pieces missing– too many to even get an accurate idea of a picture being formed. It is getting late and I open a can of soup for dinner, fill a glass with leftover wine and start to weep. It seems that I have finally burned all my bridges. As I weep, something comes over me. A light inside me is bidding me, compelling me to go to church. I delay for a time, but ultimately drive to the Episcopal Church in Amherst.

Inside, I kneel quietly on a soft pad, leaning into the wooden pew in front of me in my version of prayer. The tears are flowing; their warmth taking me back to my childhood when I wept so often alone on my bed. I begin to feel myself suffused with an enormous, overwhelming sense of grief and sadness. But at the same time, I am slowly becoming aware of the warm glow of a tremendous presence in the room—something miraculous. Whatever it is, I feel certain that it is the only thing that will never abandon me. It is a force so powerful that I can concentrate on nothing but the feeling of its presence in the room. The words tumble out of me, quietly beseeching that presence, "God help me recover. Please God, PLEASE HEAL ME."

The service is over and as people leave for their decorated, joyous homes, I am still bent into the pew in front of me, transfixed by that powerful force and begging for help. Ultimately, I am aware of being the last person there and so I stand up slowly. The minister is waiting quietly at the door to send me off with a warm handshake and a holiday wish. I go to him haltingly, gazing downwards, unwilling to show him the devastated expression that must be written all over my face. I let him shake my hand and then I quickly scurry out the door into the cold and snowy evening as he calls "Merry Christmas! Come back again soon!"

Back at the farmhouse, ignoring the bottle of vodka on the counter, I am satisfied instead to drink a diet Coke and go to bed not even suspecting that the next day—Christmas Day—will be the first day of my escape from the beast that has been devouring me.

Christmas Day, 1991. Attending a family Christmas gathering the morning after such a powerful experience in that little Amherst church, I am a miserable, quaking, shaking bundle of nerve endings. Despite this, I realize I am finally out of options. I know I have to resist the overwhelming need for more alcohol with every shred of strength and consciousness in me. Pain is shooting through my body like electric currents. I can't sit still, and I can't focus on the happy holiday conversations going on all around me. I drink gallons of tea and—desperately holding onto the cup with two uncertain, palsied hands—greedily seek another refill as soon as I gulp down the last. This time there are no tranquilizers to help me through withdrawal. There are no similarly withdrawing co-drunks with whom to banter and pretend that nothing is really wrong. I am on my own, out of options, and holding on for dear life through the monstrous never-ending avalanche of withdrawal.

Miraculously, I emerge alive and clearheaded at the other end. Shaken and unnerved, I am nevertheless certain that I have finally had my last 'last' drink. This time—for the first time—I feel an honest conviction; _I will prevail_. I will make a new life for myself that replaces alcohol with the miraculous energizing force that swept over me while I pleaded for help with my addiction.

December 25, 1991 will be my sober date for the rest of my life.

Kris

Christmas was, overall, a happy memory for me. When I was young, we spent Christmas Eve at Mom's parents' house. All my cousins would be there. It is funny that for some reason I remember the zip-up boots my mom always wore. They were out-of-date then, but seem to be in fashion today. Pop would be wearing his wide-whale corduroys and always some funky holiday tie. We all had to be dressed for the occasion because there were always obligatory pictures being taken. We kids ran through the house cleaning out the M&M bowl while the adults chatted and had a few too many cocktails. Gifts were handed out and the night at our grandparents' would end right after dinner.

Mom did a great job covering her drinking in those days, and I don't have any unpleasant memories of her slurring her words or being off-balance. When we got home, we would all sit down to read The Night before Christmas and as the oldest, I usually read the book while my siblings gathered around me. Instead of cookies and milk, we put out Pennsylvania pretzels and a cold beer for Santa, and Pop would put on the classical music station which played Christmas music through the night. Mom's rule was that stockings would be placed outside our bedrooms so that when we woke up, there they were, filled with all kinds of treats, magazines and other things for us to open before breakfast. As I look back into the Christmas traditions of our family, I chuckle because for all these years I have thought my mother placed our stockings outside our bedroom doors so that we would keep ourselves busy and let her and Pop sleep in on Christmas morning. This was a tradition that I continued with my three children when they were very young. But now I understand that it sprang from the desperation of a woman who wanted to sleep off her Christmas Eve hangovers! Those stupid light bulb moments about the myths of childhood turn on at random times; this one took just a little longer to turn on for me!

Christmas breakfast would begin after we opened our gifts. Mom put together the most amazing breakfast treats, and to this day I have carried on that tradition with my own family. Mom would have little chocolates sitting at each place setting and there would be all kinds of delicious things to eat. One thing I remember her making which I think we all still make for our own families on Christmas morning is "Cheesy Eggs."

Mom was very good at covering her tracks in the beginning of her alcoholic slide. She gave us Christmas breakfast in all its glory, including those wonderful eggs! Little did I know that our festive toast with champagne to start the day —with sparkling juice for the little kids—was to help curb my mother's alcoholic shakes. I am glad I didn't know then that Mom couldn't get through a day without alcohol. I am thankful in some ways that I was so naïve, because it protected my idea of what Christmas should be and therefore has allowed me to cherish the time and look back on so many of the happy memories our family had. But simply calling me naïve would be an understatement! When I was in fourth grade, Pop rallied a friend to call me on the phone and ask what I wanted for Christmas. The man told me he was Santa Claus and I took the bait, hook, line and sinker. Really? Santa on the phone putting together his list? Apparently, I really wanted to believe in myths still and that helped me fail to notice Mom's little problem for awhile.

As I got a bit older and stopped believing in Santa Claus, I selfishly took the dream away from my younger sister Hallie by telling her there was no Santa. This is a very vivid memory for Hallie; one that I am not proud of. Because my world was starting to change and my responsibilities were growing, I was clearly becoming an angry child. No one would have noticed that change on the surface, but deep down I guess I felt the need to take my anger out on someone. Unfortunately it was Hallie. I envied her because she was—in my mind—a happy child who didn't seem to be bothered by what was happening to our family. I felt I couldn't take my anger out on anyone else, so Hallie slowly became my target. Snatching the Christmas dream away from her was cruel and not sisterly. I obviously had issues, yet was unable to talk about my feelings with anyone. I didn't want to worry Pop, and Mom was slowly losing touch with everything around her. I loved my sister dearly and protected her for many years, but the reality of what my mom was doing to our family seemed to be driving a wedge between us.

After Mom left us, Christmas never seemed the same. Pop did his best, but he couldn't do the Christmas cheer and tradition thing on his own. He tried to include Mom but by then she was spiraling out of control and drinking heavily during the holidays. Not surprisingly, she had come to feel like an outsider or an outcast, left out of our warm family circle. I remember her telling me that at one time during the holidays she sometimes drove up to the house but at the last minute didn't stop or come in. There were times when I drove my siblings to her condo to visit but she couldn't even talk or walk. I think that began during my junior or senior year of high school when Pop was dating Jean and she was slowly taking over my mother's role at Christmas. My younger siblings were very receptive to Jean and she was good to them, but I just couldn't let her into my life; certainly not at Christmas.

A feeling of emptiness took over our house at Christmastime. Pop's mom would come and we loved having her around, but as much as we tried to duplicate the past traditions, things were just different. We still attended church as a family on Christmas Eve, Pop still put on the Christmas morning breakfast, and I continued to read The Night before Christmas out loud until I left for college. I don't think my mom wanted to continue living in those days; at least that's what it felt like. The loss of her children and the loss of her mother in 1987 must have seemed too much for her to handle. You know what? Even after all the years of heartache and sadness, my heart feels warm at Christmas and the season is still a happy time. Mom created special memories when I was young and I am grateful for that. But my sisters' memories of Christmas are darker than mine.

Lindsey: My mom made so many promises that she couldn't keep, and she let us down so many times. Holidays were especially tough. We would get ready to go over to her house, not knowing if she was dead, alive, sober or drunk. Looking back, I guess this was the case every time we called her or rang her doorbell. I would anticipate our visits/calls with such an uneasy feeling. How would she look when we opened the door? How would she behave? I was super observant and super aware of every mannerism; my daughter is the same way about me. I don't want my children to doubt their instincts when it comes to me.

As an adult, it's not that I have a hard time trusting people. It's worse than that; I don't invest myself emotionally in people 100 percent so that if they leave me/hurt me, I will be okay. I have been hardened. Now that I am a mom of two young kids, I can't imagine what it was like for my mom to leave her kids time and time again. I don't think I fully grasped it until I was a mom myself.

Hallie: On the Christmas Eve after my grandmother— Mom's mother—died, I was old enough to have my driver's license and planned to drive the little kids to visit Mom. They were all dressed up and had wrapped up the presents they made for her. They were excited to see her. But then we got a call from her then-boyfriend who said Mom was unconscious at her place. I turned to the little kids and said, "Mom has a bad cold. We'll see her in a few days when she's feeling better." Then I drove back alone to Mom's house. There were ambulances there and I was very afraid of what I would see inside the house. Mom was totally out of it—bloated and barely alive. In fact, I hardly recognized her. There was a little puppy in a crate barking and barking.

Later, when she was in the hospital, Mom couldn't even tell the doctor who I was, although I was standing right there. She didn't even recognize her own daughter! It was the worst experience of my entire life; and to make things worse, it was Christmas Eve.

We had always made a big deal of Christmas in our family. But after this experience, it took me a very long time to get excited about Christmas again.

Kris had taken off for Germany sometime before that terrible incident and stayed for several years, I suppose in part to stay away from our family situation; I admit I resented her for being gone. Mom's drinking was definitely peaking at that time and she was dishing out more abuse to me than Kris had ever experienced. It had always been Kris and me who had acted as a team and protected the younger kids from our mother's drunken behavior. Now Kris was gone and I felt completely alone in this nightmare.

CHAPTER NINE

᭣

Adjusting to Sobriety

With the end of my drinking life came a rush of doubts and questions. I realized in the most painful way that I had been blaming my disastrous life on my parents, on my brother Tom, on Ron, on my lonely childhood—whatever bullshit I could use to avoid the truth. For years, I had been judging others in terms of what they hadn't done for me—how they had failed me, victimized me. I had been living like a spoiled child, each new dream or delusion leading me to more self delusion. And worse, I had built up a nice, neat system for blaming all my failures and shortcomings on anyone but myself. When was I going to start taking control of my own life? When would I stop telling myself, *If only I weren't married... If only I were with the right man... if only, if only...* Finally, I started to kick myself in the ass. Now I was telling myself; *Do something! Be someone! Make a difference!*

All the things I had prayed for and all the power I tried to exhort from my dying mother suddenly began to come to me. I was continuously sober for the first time in many, many years and for once there was no man in my life who I could use as an excuse for not being a strong and independent woman. I resolved to get back to Smith full time and finish the degree that had eluded me for so long.

My whole life suddenly became focused on attending AA in the morning and then walking up the hill to my afternoon classes on the Smith campus. Now that I was alert enough to pay attention to my surroundings and observe intelligent, focused, and independent women in an academic setting, I even started to become a bit of a feminist. For the first time, I wondered why I had always been so dependent on men. And I wondered why I had always sought easy ways out of taking responsibility for my own life. I realized what a dependent, pathetic person I had been for so many years and thanks to AA and Smith, I began to finally take charge of my life.

Finally, I was getting a feeling for what sobriety really means and despite the shame and emotional pain I was feeling, I had a confident sense that this time, things were going to work for me. I told myself to just move forward and not think too much about my many problems. My new mantra became more complicated; *Take one day at a time, keep going, go to class, do the work, get the papers written, stay out of unhealthy relationships with men, put your life together.* Little by little, I began to gain confidence that I would not only be able to finish my Smith degree, but that I would be able go on to become a licensed therapist. For the first time in my life I could actually focus on the outline of a meaningful career and see myself as a professional person capable of helping other people beat the same scourge that had consumed me for so long.

Here's where the heroic orchestral music swelling in the background slows down to a slow, hesitant clarinet interlude and then peters out...

There was a man in AA—he was known in the group for being a bit rude and arrogant because he did crossword puzzles during the meetings; he could see that I was serious about recovery and he became interested in helping me. I felt myself becoming attracted to him. Paul was an unmarried, devout Catholic who lived with his mother. He was a few years younger than I was, a professional career man, and a popular guy around town who had been sober for a couple of years. He took me under his wing and began accompanying me to AA meetings regularly.

At first, I appreciated Paul's need for structure and his total immersion in the rules and tenets of AA; it gave me a degree of confidence in our growing relationship and a feeling that I had someone knowledgeable and strong to lean on. He helped me move out of the farmhouse I had shared with Bill, got me back into my place in Amherst, and was very kind and good to me. I loved the idea of having a stable person in my life and thought that if I were with Paul, my kids would see that I had finally made a smart decision—that I was finally with an AA man who had an actual job. It seemed that everyone who knew me was breathing a sigh of relief.

I was sober and in early recovery and was getting a lot of help at Smith with the learning difficulties that had plagued me all my life. Now I was receiving a new, positive message from my academic experience and told myself; *You are a smart person with good ideas and a natural aptitude for psychology; you just need a good typist and a lot of help with the mechanics of learning and test-taking!*

Paul was eager to marry me and I kind of slid into our engagement, knowing that I wasn't in love with him and probably never would be. As usual, I was not honest with him, so he naturally assumed that I returned his affection. This passivity was the familiar irresponsible, childish side of me. He had given me an engagement ring and that was that; I would marry him. Clearly, I still hadn't reached the point where I could maintain my independence when I was with a man who wanted to be with me.

In AA, there is an expression, "taking people hostage in your life." This is what I was doing to Paul. I didn't really want most of the men I had allowed into my life, but they all served some sort of purpose for me and I simply allowed myself to get sucked into relationships with them. I guess that kind of behavior gave me a form of control in my life—I could control my sex life in a way I couldn't control many other things—especially drinking. Paul had no idea that I didn't love him. He was a nice guy from a hard-working blue collar family who had gone to an excellent college and become successful in his career. He didn't have a clue what he was getting into with me. I was free of my addiction to alcohol, but in so very many ways, I was damaged goods.

While I was engaged to Paul, I took a year's leave from Smith to take a coveted internship at Hazelden Treatment Center in

Minnesota. During that time I lived in a small town of 500 and rented a cozy cabin on a lake. I was very happy living by myself and staying sober while nestled comfortably in the close Hazelden community. When Paul flew out to visit me on the weekends, I found that I resented his presence and looked forward impatiently to the end of each visit. I should have realized that this was a sign that our marriage was a bad idea. But like many feelings I was experiencing, I simply ignored them. I wanted to make things work. Once again, my passivity with men overshadowed any better instincts I might have followed. Above all, I wanted to be alone so that I could continue to develop into a mature and independent person and acquire some of the skills of a profession I could see myself entering. But I didn't bother to let Paul know that. I regret that he was an innocent victim of my continuing inability to identify, understand and communicate my needs or act like a mature adult.

I graduated from Smith in May of 1995. In doing so, I may have established a college record for the amount of time it took to finish a BA degree, but I was no less proud of myself than the most accomplished graduate that day! My two brothers showed up for the ceremony and stood applauding enthusiastically as I marched past them with the rest of the graduating class. I was filled with the excitement of all the possibilities that had opened up before me. In a way, this graduation symbolized my rebirth.

Paul and I got married that summer and soon after we bought a split level house in a town near Northampton. Life was good enough and we continued to attend AA together and support each other's sobriety. But we had very different ideas about how to participate in AA. In his mind, if you weren't following the AA rules to the letter, you weren't in a state of sobriety. I knew I needed the basic structure that AA gave me in my life, but I was more eclectic in the ways I bolstered my sobriety. And Paul became increasingly critical of the things I said in the meetings. Knowing that he was listening with a critical ear to everything I said, I began to hate going to meetings with him. I no longer felt I could share my thoughts honestly while he was there, ready to pounce on my unorthodox expressions of feeling and emotion and my need for independence from what I began to view as 'drunk dogma.' As the tension began to build, I started to think of our marriage as just another of my many mistakes.

I was extremely grateful for my AA experience, but I observed an unattractive neediness—even a cult-like obedience—in some of the participants and did not want that for myself. I wanted to use the strength I had gained to become more self-reliant and outgoing in a larger circle. That meant seeking new inspiration and ideas outside of AA. But Paul made it clear that he didn't like my patchwork brand of sobriety and continued to be very critical of me.

Through all my crises—certainly throughout my struggle to achieve sobriety—I continued to wrestle with alcohol's twin addiction, bulimia. It seemed that I had long been consumed by one or another of the two evil twins. A person can be sober after being besotted with alcohol, but still be struggling with the same emotional demons that kept the alcohol abuse going for so long—in my case, the demons were depression, anxiety and shame. Now that I was sober, the bulimia took over as my primary coping mechanism—my way of comforting myself at times of stress and uncertainty. Just as the alcohol addiction had completely taken over my identity, the bulimia now subsumed my personality and made it difficult for me to carry on a normal relationship with Paul. Although I wasn't drinking alcohol and was going to AA on a regular basis, I still had to deal with my feelings of shame and anxiety. To do this, I was eating large amounts of food and purging regularly.

Paul did not know about the bulimia, but he was aware that I took laxatives frequently because of a longstanding intestinal disorder and assumed that the laxatives were tied to an earlier eating disorder. But he really had no idea how strongly the bulimia had returned after I successfully stopped drinking. Despite this ongoing secret struggle, I was working on my professional future which had become extremely important to me.

After my graduation, I worked at the Institute Of Living—the very same place where I had been a very sick patient several times—in an amazing, prestigious job in the substance abuse program. But the daily commute was arduous and I eventually found a job closer to home, at the Bay State Hospital in Springfield. It seemed that finally I was on my way. Within two years after my graduation from Smith, I knew I was ready to tackle graduate school at Springfield College.

I was accepted in the Marriage and Family Therapy program and for two years I worked hard to get a graduate degree. Smith had taught me how to study, had given me the confidence and the tools and techniques needed to deal with my learning difficulties, and I was highly interested in the material I was studying. These positives—and the fact that I was now working my ass off—made me an excellent, dedicated graduate student, focused on a professional career. In addition, I continued to go to AA meetings at night. In the end, I had to pass a national exam for the M.Ed. degree and did well. The fact that I knew the material cold had magically overtaken my longstanding difficulties with test-taking.

Now for the best miracle of all the miracles that happened in those first sober years; Courtney decided to come and live with me for a time. This would be the first time in many years I had the joy and privilege of living with any of my children. I was filled with hope. When she arrived, it seemed to me that she held the key to opening up my true feelings—mainly that I was no longer happy with Paul.

I loved having Courtney living with me and just couldn't get enough of it. She and I did everything together. But Paul began acting out his resentment about our newfound mother-daughter relationship in a number of passive-aggressive ways. Also, while I was helping Courtney find a place to live, the more I helped her look, the more I realized I wanted to get out of my marriage to Paul.

Paul and I had been married for about five years when we began to argue frequently and viciously. I remember canceling a planned Thanksgiving dinner because of a particularly heated exchange and the residue of blame and recrimination which hung over our house afterward. The fact is that we had begun to thoroughly dislike one another. To my growing list of complaints about him, I added his jealousy towards Courtney and his controlling, arrogant manner towards me. I knew that he needed approval and recognition for what he had done to help me stay sober, but I was no longer in the frame of mind to be his grateful subject. As my self confidence grew, my regard for him dropped precipitously. I can only assume he felt equally negative about me.

When I attended a marriage and family therapy conference in Chicago, I called the director of the downtown Hazelden addiction unit to tell her I wanted to talk to her about working there. She told me they were looking for a counselor on the residential unit. Ultimately, she offered me the job and I jumped at the opportunity.

When I got home, I said to Paul that I really wanted to take the job. He said, "You can't. We're married." I said without dropping the beat, "Well, I'm going. If you want, you can move to Chicago after I get settled." Paul was happy living in Massachusetts where he had family and friends, and the notion of moving to Chicago left him cold. Despite his obvious discomfort and my own misgivings, I packed up some of my things and put them in my Honda for the trip. When I walked out the door, I left my beloved Beagles, Ben and Bruno, sleeping on the couch. At that moment, I felt that it was harder to part with those two dogs than it was to leave Paul behind.

Once again, I had bolted from a relationship, leaving a messy trail of belongings and unfinished business. I was terrified and excited at the same time. I had never lived in a big city like Chicago and cried a good deal of the time as I drove the nearly three-day trip alone. I called Paul several times along the way and admitted to him I wasn't sure this move was a good idea. He replied sullenly, "Well, you gotta do what you gotta do," and in response, I felt a newfound resolve to live alone. I remember confiding in my brother Bruce about the situation with Paul. He said, "Well, maybe you have outgrown him," and then he pointed out that I now had two degrees which would help me move forward on my own.

When I moved into my big apartment on North Dearborn, I was very excited and determined to do well. I went to AA meetings every day, met people, and became fully involved in a professional routine at Hazelden. Paul came to visit me in and found to his surprise that Chicago was a place where he could see himself living happily. When he told me he was willing to move there so we could be together again, I had to confront the hard truth; I didn't want him to move to Chicago. I didn't want him to enter my new world. I didn't even want to be married to him. And so, when we said goodbye after his short visit, it was for good.

Hurting Paul in this way was cruel treatment for someone who did not deserve it. But AA teaches you to "put your recovery first" and I told myself that I was doing just that. I knew I had been living a lie by staying with him. The opportunity for me to be in Chicago alone and improve my chances for a successful life was a huge one for me.

Looking back on my lies, rationalizations and cruelties toward Paul, I went back to Massachusetts many years later to make amends to him. We met briefly in a coffee shop and I saw immediately that he was still a very angry man. He was barely able to listen to my words and as soon as he could, he quickly excused himself and left without ceremony.

Not unexpectedly, with so many changes and challenges in my life, I became depressed for a while after moving to Chicago, but found a great therapist who helped me climb out of the problem. A thrilling side effect of becoming an independent woman while I was living and working in Chicago was that I was able to stop smoking and then miraculously dropped the bulimia addiction for good. Now that I was fully embarked on a private journey of Recovery, I tried never to look back over my shoulder at those dark guilt-ridden shadows lurking in my past.

Kris

Courtney's reconnection with Mom in Amherst was relatively smooth except for the Paul part. But for me personally, there was more of the bad Mom story to go before things got better.

Courtney: It took a while for me to really reconnect with mom because I was wary for a long time, thinking that she would relapse. I had gotten used to the roller-coaster of emotions that occurred with my mom, to a point where feelings of disappointment, hurt, distrust, hope, sadness had made me numb and I was always expecting her to fall off the wagon. It certainly would not have been a surprise if she did. So for the first years of her sobriety there was still distance between us. I just didn't allow myself to trust her; anticipating her failure to stay sober would at least protect me from feeling disappointed again.

My reconnection was a gradual thing but it really started when I moved back east to the town where she was living. I had been living in Charleston, South Carolina, where I graduated from college. I had thought I'd stay in Charleston forever—it was peaceful and sunny and I didn't have to deal with my parents. It wasn't Mom I was hiding from at that time; it was my dad and his second wife, my stepmom. Their marriage had been falling apart for years and it was hard to be around them. When I heard news about them divorcing I let out a sigh of relief and suddenly found that I wanted to return home again; not to the home I once knew, where my father lived, but to a new home—one I had never really experienced—where Mom was living. I was craving a new start, and motherly love—something I had been without for a long time. I found that I missed Mom, in a true heartfelt way. I wanted to re-connect with her— to give us a chance to be a mother and daughter. So I packed up my car and hit the road, leaving Charleston behind. Without much forethought, I moved in with my mom and her husband—much to his dismay and discomfort. My mom was thrilled—I could feel it.

I felt so happy; my plan was to stay with Mom until I got my feet on the ground and found my own place. I stayed with her for maybe a month and she helped me find my own apartment, only a few miles away. But while my stay with Mom was a very bonding experience for us, I could sense the obvious tension it caused between Paul and Mom. He was clearly not comfortable with me in his space, and he did not like sharing with me his time with Mom. He was jealous and moody. I did not fault him; he had never fathered any of children of his own, and probably did not truly understand that bond. He started acting like a spoiled child, deprived of attention. I knew my mom was not happy with her relationship with him, but I could see that it provided a safe place for her—the two had met at AA and were keeping each other sober.

I was thrilled to be living near Mom—I was extremely happy and my heart felt free. Finally, I felt complete in my life and knew that my mom was truly there for me. While I was very happy with the new chapter I had started with my life, with the help of my mom, I knew deep inside that she herself was not happy living with Paul, and in a town that had so many painful memories for her.

When Mom helped me hunt for an apartment, she said she was jealous because she would love to be looking for her own place too. I knew then that I might lose her again. But I also knew that I wanted the best for her and wanted her to find her own true happiness and independence. I realized that mom needed something more for herself, but I must admit I wasn't quite ready so soon or so abruptly. Then Mom went out to Chicago for a work event or something—and she called to announce she was going to move there. I was so torn. Was she leaving me again so soon after we finally reconnected and were living in the same town as mother and daughter for the first time? I had to dig into my heart and soul to realize that *No*, she wasn't leaving me. She was leaving an unhealthy relationship with her husband, for a life she so deserved—a life of independence, free of dependence on a man, free of a town filled with bad memories. It seemed she was letting go in order to find her true self. And she did! That was the best move of her entire life—it shaped the person she is today. She created a life of JANE—a healthy happy Jane. What more could a daughter want for her mom? I was so-o-o proud of her.

Initially I was worried that this move would affect the mother-daughter-friend bond that we had finally created, but I was wrong. After she left, Mom called me every week to check in. She stayed connected with me and I felt her presence. She was reliable now. She flew me out to visit whenever I needed a Mom fix. She said she would be there for me if I ever needed a thing. And I finally believed her. While she regained her own life, I was included in it. Maybe it was because I let her include me, maybe it was because I let myself include her. I don't know how it happened, but it did. I got my mom back, and that's all that matters. The rest is history.

It was obvious that Mom wasn't happy with Paul and needed a reason to leave him. That's what she did best; settle into something for a while and then flee, leaving a messy trail behind. I know she realized that she had made a mistake in marrying Paul and clearly she was very thankful to have Courtney come to live in Amherst after so many years of little or no contact. But basically, it was clear to me that Mom was feeling a strong need to run again. According to our history with her, Mom's decisions were always selfish ones. Nevertheless, I was thrilled at the idea of my mom moving to Chicago, close to me and my kids. I didn't judge her reasons, didn't want to argue over why she came to

Chicago, and was hopeful that she and I finally would be able to build on our interrupted relationship.

I was going through a rough time in my own marriage and I really needed to have my mother present. Mom was sober and on a healthy track, so it seemed like perfect timing for her to use that therapy degree to help me figure out my own life. After Paul's visit to Chicago, Mom told me her third marriage was over and I suggested that she needed to stay away from men for a while. She agreed that she needed to spend some time alone and get her feet wet while launching a career. Well, that didn't last long! Before I knew it, she was going out on dates and met another guy at her AA meetings. This is where the happy story of Jane getting her life on track takes a nasty turn.

Mom digs into her job at Hazelden and I am finally proud to say that she seems to be getting stronger. This all comes crashing down on us though, because while my mom is working in Chicago, she is attempting to put herself out there to find a new mate. We visit and talk often—and my kids get to know her. Overall, things seem like they are heading in the right direction, but I am concerned about the choices she is making about men. While she is sober and claiming to be happy, I am seeing something a little different. Mom was never very long without a man, so she starts hanging out with this guy Rob who she met in an AA meeting in downtown Chicago. Rob is charming and can talk about anything. The problem is that he appears to be a pathological liar. My husband questions everything about him—his motives, his integrity, his stories, and even his identity.

At first Rob seems charming. He makes Mom laugh and my kids seem to think he is a nice guy. Mom is living alone in the city and I know she is struggling to follow my advice about spending time alone, but Rob is pressuring her to spend more time with him. She is now trying to keep everyone happy, but I know she secretly wants to get rid of Rob. Then suddenly, she does what she always does—finds an escape route. This time, she decides to move closer to me and my family.

Mom finds an adorable house near me and moves out of the city. I am excited that my kids will spend more time with her. Mom's house oozes her personality and seems like the perfect fit for her. I keep telling myself that Mom will be able to help me out if I can't save my marriage.

Parents don't know how much power they have over us. We all want to feel loved and don't want to disappoint our parents. I keep telling myself; At least I will have my mom by my side. And then comes Rob!

I'm sure that establishing distance seems to Mom like a perfect way to get rid of Rob, but he just won't go away. The first mistake is letting him come and hang out with her and my family for a day. Why is my mom so weak? Hasn't she been listening to what my husband and I have been telling her about Rob? After her move out of the city, he becomes more determined to be with her. I try to help her work up the strength to break up with him, but in reality she is just telling me what I want to hear and not telling Rob what he doesn't want to hear! I am thinking, How can she become a therapist and help other people when she can't help herself? Eventually, she reveals that she has been getting increasingly nervous about Rob and that he is beginning to talk obsessively about them being together forever.

Now the story gets really ugly and I'm sure this chapter in her life is one she would like to erase. I realize this crazed man is becoming more than Mom can handle. My mother can't seem to get rid of her crazy suitor and my husband is furious about the situation. I become the pawn being pulled back and forth between my mother and my husband and Rob is showing up repeatedly, making everything that much worse. Now I am begging Mom to level with Rob and get him out of our lives. We are singing a familiar duet; I am once again the mother of my own mother.

Rob manages to get a job volunteering for the local high school football team and starts looking for a place to live in our community. Soon, even the football coaches start to question his stories and they let him go. I talk to Hallie about my issues with mom but she is far away. I can't really talk to my husband about the situation, because he is done with Mom and makes me feel defensive about her. I want to prove to him that she is getting better, yet there is nothing to stand on. Mom is digging her grave deeper and deeper with each poor decision she makes.

Mom finally gets serious and tries to break up with Rob, but he won't stop coming around. He threatens her by doing things like leaving on her doorstep smashed photos of the two of them together. Eventually, he leaves wrecked photos just of her. If he can't be with her, he says, no one else will be either! We encourage my mom to go the police, and *she files a report. Nevertheless, Rob is getting scarier by the moment and won't leave us alone. As things are getting uglier, my mother meets someone new and falls for him! The new guy is Don, an Economics professor at the University of Wisconsin.*

Now, guess who is leaving town! You guessed it, my mother. This is where I turn into a very pissed-off daughter who is about to snap! My anger, sadness and troubles are growing, I am feeling helpless and cursed and it is all about Mom again! In her haste to get away from Rob and be with her new man, Mom quickly sells her house and prepares to leave me to deal with her psycho ex-boyfriend. Rob starts blaming my husband and me for the failure of his relationship with Mom. He even calls my husband at work accusing him of breaking them up and threatening to harm him. My husband has now reached his breaking point. Any healthy person would clean up their mess before moving on. But Mom doesn't even seem to notice what she is leaving behind. Now I begin to worry about my children playing outside without me around. This guy will do anything to keep my mom in his life. I am going to sleep thinking I have lost my mind. Way to go, Mom!

My husband and I lie awake at night worrying that Rob will break into our house and shoot us! One day Mom stops by the house and I can't stand to even look at her. I shout at her, "Look what you have done to us!" At that moment, I don't care what Rob might do to her and I certainly don't want her in my life; she is still just too screwed up. Finally, I look her in the eyes and tell her that she is no longer welcome in my house. Further, I don't want to see or talk to her again.

It was a horrible time. After all the time and all the things our family had been through because of her drinking and bad judgment, I had thought Mom would be smarter and would know how to do the right thing. But she disappointed me again. I stared at my mom and felt all the hurt and anger accumulated over the years when I told her to leave. She was a broken person when she left, and we didn't speak for months.

Here is the clincher; I found out that Rob was going to tour my neighbor's house which was on the market. I knew he couldn't afford that house and it seemed that this was another ploy to scare us and remind us that he was lurking around, planning his next move. I advised my neighbor to let Rob come to see the house. While another neighbor kept a close eye on my children, I saw Rob's car arrive and watched him go inside the house. Suddenly, I didn't care what he might do to me and I marched down the street and stood in front of his car waiting for him to emerge from the house. Rob was a big brawny man and certainly wouldn't have been afraid of me or even expected to see me blocking his car door. But I stood there without flinching. When he walked toward me, I noticed that he couldn't make eye contact.

I got in his face and told him that he didn't scare me (total lie) and I would be watching him closely from now on. I explained that if I ever saw him anywhere near my neighborhood I would have the police drag him down to the station. I also told him that my mother wasn't worth his time. My eyes and my body language said it all. I wasn't going to let him get into his car until I was through with my tirade. Moments later, when he left, I was shaking like a leaf but thankful that I found the strength to confront him. After that day, I saw him only once, riding his bike in town. He was a sad excuse for a man and all I could do was shake my head about my mother's continuing poor choices.

Time went on and eventually my mom and I started to get back on track. She told me about her new guy in Madison, Wisconsin and all I could think about was, "Here we go again!" But Mom was different with Don. She finally seemed to be at peace and appeared genuinely happy. When I began to see that my mother was really changing, our relationship started to mend and grow. She was finally there for me as I faced the failure of my own marriage. Then Mom witnessed a horrible fight between my husband and me and attempted to come to my aid. As she did so, my husband viciously attacked her with a verbal rant. When I heard what he was saying to her, I knew for sure that my marriage was over. My mother had certainly had more than her share of problems, but I felt she didn't deserve verbal abuse like that.

After that unpleasant scene, my mother became more available to me emotionally. She wanted to forget about Rob and that entire chapter, but I made her talk about it because she had created a horrible mess for me and my family and I was having a hard time getting over it. Talking honestly about that episode in our lives made it easier for me to forgive her eventually and move on. Over time, Mom slowly reclaimed her role as my mother and I felt the power of forgiveness which eased the memories of the past and filled the future with hope. Now I can *agree with Courtney's comment about her reconciliation with Mom: "The rest is history."*

CHAPTER TEN

Ꙩ

Redemption in Reconnection

I never told myself that my children would come back to me or forgive me in any way and I didn't even dare hope for that. After all, I had a great deal of trouble forgiving myself for the things I did in my addicted life. But after I became sober for good, I started trying to live a life of hard work, dedication and professionalism in the hope that I could somehow develop some self respect and find meaning in my existence. In the process, my children started coming back to me in their own time and in their own ways.

Back in 1989, before I had overcome alcoholism, I felt that Kris needed me and I saw an opportunity to help her. When she graduated from college, she was so tired of all the difficult family issues that she went to Madrid. I think she had a moment of truth and just took off. While there, she fell in love with a Canadian military man and moved to Germany to live with him. Everyone became quite worried about her, and I flew over there intending to bring her home. The two were staying in a tiny apartment and when I arrived, I made a point of staying with them so I could get a feel for the situation. Although Kris did not know it, I was still drinking at the time, but was concealing it. I was trying to be a mom again and wanted to take her home; away from this crude boyfriend. When I met him, I thought to myself, "This guy is probably going to kill me for trying to influence Kris." He was a tough guy, often spewing verbal abuse at her without hesitation— and I told Kris that she hadn't graduated from college to step into that kind of lifestyle. I encouraged her to leave him, and we talked about getting him out of her life and her out of Germany.

From that moment, I felt that Kris and I began to have a much closer relationship although I did not fool myself that she trusted me. For all those earlier years of my addiction, she had been trying to save me. Now I wanted to save her from her own bad choices. And I believed that she was glad that I wanted to help her find the strength to get out of an uncomfortable situation. When she came back with me to the states, she went to Chicago and got on with her life. Kris is like me in that her relationships with men have not always been healthy and she has been prone to getting involved with controlling men. However, unlike me she has been a consistently present and dedicated mother to her three children.

Even after I was able to stay sober, I was still making some strange decisions about men and was compulsive and reactive in many ways, often throwing caution to the wind. Thirty years of addiction doesn't just go away! I was still struggling to find the person I was meant to be and to make that person present in all my relationships and in my behavior. The second part of Kris' story of reconnection—the one that occurred when I brought my own messy relationship with a guy called Rob into her life—is still almost too painful and embarrassing for me to remember or write about.

Courtney was the first to identify her visceral need for a relationship with her natural mother and her move to Amherst to be with me seems to have broken the ice. My slow reconnection with Kris was—like so many things in my life—marred by my inability to act like a reasonable adult. Despite my own errors and weaknesses, I thoroughly embraced the willingness of both Kris and Courtney to forgive me and considered their return to my life a miraculous gift. The other three children, in their own ways and in their own time, re-entered my life as well. Maybe they saw what happened with Kris and Courtney and began to believe that I had indeed overcome my terrible addiction to alcohol and that maybe I was worthy of their reconsideration.

Tyler had a harder time connecting with me after all those years during which I caused my family so much continued heartbreak, and he still chooses not to use the word forgiveness when he talks about our relationship. For him the breakthrough came when I invited him to accompany Don and me to China a few years ago. I didn't know what would happen but I knew that Tyler has always been fascinated by China and I hoped he would overcome his hesitation and go with us. He and I were awkward with each other at the beginning of the trip; he needed to tell me how angry he was about my past and I needed to tell him that I thought those feelings were necessary and okay with me.

Tyler is like me in that we often have trouble with a sense of direction, and when we went out together to explore Nanjing, we quickly became lost. Eventually we started to laugh about being lost, and as we laughed together, we began to feel more comfortable. Suddenly we just started talking about things we had never talked about before. After all, he had seldom seen me sober!

Tyler later told some of his friends that the experience of reconnecting with his mother in China was life-changing. But I know that most of his other memories of me are very bittersweet. He was the baby, and he used to stand in the driveway and wave goodbye to me and cry as I drove out of his life for long periods of time. And I broke many promises I made to him. I recently talked to him about the story Ron told earlier about Tyler sitting on the front step waiting for me and I never came. In talking to him about this shameful incident, I couldn't help but break down weeping. Tyler was emotionally affected by my obvious and deep sorrow and I felt that because of it we came even closer together. Although he internalizes his feelings a lot and has never spoken harshly to me for what I did to him, he is a talented writer and I hope he will be able to use his writing talent to dispel some of the demons that still lurk in his memory of the past.

My sons-in-law have wondered how my daughters have been able to forgive me. They have been surprised that my children don't hate me for the things I did that disrupted their lives and showered misery on them. And I think there have been times when they worried that their wives might become too much like me. But, miraculously, they too have come to a place of affection and understanding. This is amazing to me. I am upfront now; I don't want anyone to have secrets any more. I don't want my grandchildren to carry on those secret feelings and knowledge about the past. I want the truth to be out there—to set us free! Nothing can be worse than the way things used to be with me, and I tell my children this to encourage them to say whatever they want to say, especially whatever they have hesitated to say in the past.

The older kids remember when we used to have picnics in the living room, and how we used to laugh and do silly things together. The younger kids just don't have any memory of a healthy mother. They got me on my dark side. Hallie makes up lost time by calling me Mommy today. She says she wants to call me that because she likes having me back in her life. After all, she and Kris lost both their father and their mother. Ron is the constant in their lives, but I am working hard to make up for the problems I caused all of them. The hard part is realizing what kind of person I was in those days—a person I don't even know any more.

Kris

When I graduated from high school, I thought; Yes! Now, I can get away from all this family drama and start my own life. In many ways I was emotionally and socially behind my peers and couldn't think beyond just getting my college degree. I assumed I would eventually figure out what to do with my life.

After graduating from college, I was given the opportunity to travel in Europe with some friends for a few weeks. Before leaving for Europe, I had an argument with Pop. He had taken me aside and said, "Kristina, you are now on your own. We will be here for you emotionally, but financially we are done."

Really? I had no clue what I was going to do with my degree and now suddenly I was on my own! I was scared to death. I had only a month to figure things out, and I needed some help. I knew it wasn't an option to talk to Mom about my fears because she and I were not even connected then. I know Pop thought he was helping me become a strong independent woman. He wanted me to get the message that it was now time for me to 'fly', but he had no idea how fragile I was, or how lost. After all, it had always been my habit to put on a brave face and tell him what he wanted to hear.

As my trip oversees neared the end, I dreaded what I thought of as doomsday—the day I would have to return home. I felt sorry for myself and wondered, Why was Pop still supporting Mom but planning to cut me off when I'm not ready to face the world and become an adult? During the last week in Europe I missed my train to Paris and decided to travel by myself for the remainder of the time and then meet up with everyone at the airport. In a split second decision which I think of as 'pulling a Mom', I met a group of vacationing Canadians in the south of Spain and was easily talked into jumping in a car with these 7 strangers and heading back to Germany where they were stationed with the Army. In the meantime, my poor friends waited and waited for me to show up at the train station. I never gave any thought to the possibility that they might be worried about me!

I had made a decision to remain in Germany with my new friends and not go back home to the U.S. I figured I was already going to be cut off from my family, so why not escape and start a new life, one without dysfunction, alcoholism and virtually no guidance? I called Grandma when I made my decision because no one else was answering the phone. Then Pop called me back. He asked, "How much money do you have left?" And when I told him, he answered, "Good luck because that is all you'll have from me!"

Ouch! Now I am thinking I'm going to be dead meat if I return to the states, so I'd better settle into my new life in Germany and find a job quickly. I was the one being irresponsible now and it actually felt good! I was tired of being the responsible oldest child who was always there, never causing trouble, holding in so much sadness and loss, always worried about everything! Like my mother, this time I just ran away from a problem I couldn't bear to face.

Fast forward to Mom coming to Germany for a visit; at this stage, I am settled in a relationship with a hot-tempered guy and we are newly engaged. I'm thinking now I really don't have to go back home—ever. We're going to live far away in Newfoundland! But I'm unhappy in the relationship and miss my family tremendously. Somehow I choose to pretend happiness about being with a man I don't love! Sounds like a page torn out of Mom's book, doesn't it?

Mom was eager to prove to everyone that she was strong and present in our lives so she decided to visit me in Germany, talk some sense into me, and persuade me to come home. Needless to say my fiancé was not pleased about Mom's visit and he unleashed his ruthless temper while I tried to defend her. I trusted her promise that she had stopped drinking but he argued that she was even drunk during the visit. I should have known she was still drinking because I put her on a tour one day and she ended up in the wrong country! I had wanted to believe she was doing better.

Things changed one day when Mom looked at me and said, "If you love this guy, I will help you put together a wedding." Wow…….. this was something real, something honest coming from my mother! I looked at her and suddenly blurted out that I didn't want to marry the guy but I didn't know what to do. It was a healing moment for mom and me. She just took charge and after several unpleasant, heated arguments with my fiancé announced that she and I would be heading home. Everyone was elated that I was finally returning home and Mom *got the credit for helping me through a difficult time— a first for her as far as I could tell. As a result, I trusted this was the new improved Mom, the mother I had needed for such a long time. As it turned out, there was still a rocky road ahead for Mom and me, but nevertheless I will always be thankful to her for what she did for me during that troubled time in Germany.*

Hallie: I remember once hearing a quote about children wanting their mothers to be the mother bear which protects and loves them. I never felt that way with my mother, although I yearned for this to be the case. But when my son Colby was born, he was colicky and I was having a lot of postpartum problems—emotional ups and downs. Mom was the first person to show up to help me. Miraculously, she became a mother to me when I was quite vulnerable. I remember she brought me toast with jelly and a banana. It seems like not very much, but that simple motherly act was a turning point in our relationship. She was giving of herself to me for the first time I could remember in many, many years, and I started calling her *Mommy.* That was over six years ago, and I am still calling her that.

My feelings of never feeling really loved totally messed me up with men in my dating years. I found it very hard to trust and I still feel like I haven't totally overcome the need to protect myself. I love and trust my husband, but would I be surprised if he strayed? I just have this uncertainty about such things. I never trust myself to completely open up and be raw with him. I only allow this kind of openness with my children. I hug and kiss them all the time. Courtney is the only one of my mother's girls who is touchy feely and affectionate with men. But she had us to protect her from the harsh reality. Lindsey and I are the fire ants of the four girls.

Lindsey: Mom and I got close after my divorce. My entire family was mad at me for divorcing my husband because they loved him and felt that I betrayed him when, after marrying him, I realized I loved someone else. But Mom hung in there with me. When I needed my dad, he was not talking to me because of my divorce. So Mom was the only parent I could depend on and was unconditional in her support. She understood. When I was depending on Mom throughout my divorce, she gave me objective advice and stuck with me. I saw firsthand what an effective therapist she is.

At that point, Mom had been sober for a while, and I trusted her this time. When she was drinking I couldn't ever trust her. Dad was sensitive to my husband's position because—like Dad's situation with Mom—there wasn't anything he could do to get me back. I put myself in therapy and used it as my tool to gain an understanding about why I had unresolved feelings for an old boyfriend. I was married to my best friend in the world, we had traveled the world together, and yet I still longed to be with someone else. I am now with the other man—Matt, who is the father of my children—but I refuse to marry him.

The men in our lives are fearful that we all have a lot of Mom in us. When we go, we just get up and go—like Mom.

We each let Mom back in our lives at our own speed. We all just took each other's lead and we didn't push Tyler. We just let things happen organically. My father has always said, "You only have one mother." Letting her back into our lives has benefited us. You don't forget the past. We don't forget, we forgive and we have given her a place in our family.

Tyler: I can't say that I've ever truly forgiven my mother. I don't know that I'll ever know what true forgiveness is, and there will likely always be a vein of resentment running through me. However, I feel that I've been able to separate those feelings for the sake of developing a true friendship/relationship. I've been inspired by the consistency of my mom's presence in all of our lives since her recovery.

I have no memory of living with my mom, so I've always felt that we've got the most ground to make up. In my mind, it hasn't been as much about re-establishing a relationship as it has been about launching one. We were very fortunate to get an opportunity about 6 or 7 years ago to go to China together. It was the most amount of time that I could ever recall spending with my mom (about 2 weeks). We both identify this window of time as the real "game changer" for us. In travel you get to see the best of, worst of, and most authenticity in a person—we couldn't help but be real with one another. This was our time to get away from familiar spots like Amherst, Farmington, Chicago, West Hartford, Tunxis, and Key West and set out on our own adventure. We came back changed people and that was an experience that truly helped us launch!

I know that there are significant elements of my mom alive in me. We share very similar senses of humor and an appreciation of the offbeat and bizarre. Although I do like to be social, I also need my own moments of introversion and withdrawal—I think all of her kids have that aspect, whereas my father is 98% social and only likes to withdraw once in a while to recharge his battery or read a newspaper. I know that I can be emotionally difficult, as my wife will be quick to point out, and that's directly a result of my having to learn to shut down my own emotions at a young age. I also think that I inherited much of my mother's resiliency—we all did. To our collective credit, her kids have done an incredible job managing through some very painful and tumultuous years.

I am and hope to continue to be an active participant in my own daughter's life, for as long as I live. I know that I was a victim of a rather extreme circumstance; to go from an alcoholic mother, to an equally dysfunctional alcoholic stepmother was something that is beyond a child's control. However, I know there were certain aspects of my youth, even out of the hardship, that had positive results and outcomes. While there were times of feeling lonely, I never felt alone. I always felt loved and protected by my siblings, father and other extended family members. I also know that there were dysfunctional elements of my mom's marriage to my dad, and his marriage to my stepmom. The biggest lesson I've learned is that my wife and I need to stay equally committed to one another, as we are to our daughter. It's the only way that we can all share a life as a true family!

Thankfully, Mom's relationship with Don was a really good thing and still is. My kids and I liked him right away and we saw that Mom really enjoyed his company. I could see he was a normal, happy man, unlike so many of her men.

When Mom settled in Madison to be with Don, we were able to forge a new and stronger relationship; we became a team. Prior to Don, I questioned whether our mother/daughter relationship could be salvaged. Mom finding herself, finding love and earning her way back into our lives turned things around for me. She seemed to be in a different place—a much better place—and she really became available to help me deal with my divorce. She was there for me, listened to me and I felt like I really had my mom back. I needed her and she didn't back down from that responsibility.

Don has helped Mom become a better person and we are all very blessed to have him in our lives. I am so proud of who my mom has become. It may seem odd that I would say that about her, but despite all the heartache and pain I suffered by not having her present in my life, she and I are now a great team and finally in sync. Mom has grown in so many ways. I am proud of her now despite everything. I am relieved that we have been able to talk about a lot of all the hurts and disappointments she caused.

How lucky I am! These days I get to see my mother in a whole new light after many years of seeing her in a dark place and at her worst. It was so easy for me to pretend I didn't need a mother until I became one myself. Now I understand how much power there is in being a mother. I think that as parents ourselves, my siblings and I have probably overcompensated for the things that were lacking in our own lives. Would I wish on my worst enemy the pain we all felt because of my mother's addiction? No! But oddly enough, I believe that my siblings and I learned a tremendous amount about love, compassion and empathy because of the things we went through when our mother was sick; and now we are the better for it despite the scars we bear.

So many kids are raised in dysfunctional homes; I am happy to report that people can move beyond a painful past. I never thought there would be a reason for me to tell my mom truthfully how proud I am of her. I wrote her off for many years; now I cannot imagine life without her! It took her an awfully long time to get her shit together, but she did. My advice is, don't hold grudges forever. My siblings and I are living proof that love is strong and the bond of a mother and child is even stronger!

CHAPTER ELEVEN

ଚ

The Person I was Meant to Be

Today I am very busy making up for the thirty years I spent as a drunk. On a personal level, I have been engaged in a daily healing process involving my five children who have seen me at my worst and their eleven children who, thankfully, have never seen their grandmother as a drunk and a failure. I am married to my fourth husband, Don, a successful professor of Economics at the University of Wisconsin, now retired, who never knew me as a drunk and who might be shocked by the details of my life story as it unfolds in this book.

In my professional life, I am very busy. I see 15-20 clients during most weeks and also facilitate a Women's Recovery group every week. Among the clients I see individually, the main reasons for therapy are substance abuse, depression, anxiety disorders, marriage or relationship problems, eating disorders, and/ or gambling, to name a few. I work with families that have been severely affected by a loved one's addictions, and I perform couples counseling for the same problem. I run a bi-weekly group— called Women in Transition—which helps women who are going through divorce, leaving or entering the work force, or who are, as one of my clients calls it, "mothers of fucked-up kids."

I am a therapist at two outpatient clinics, Connections Counseling and The Psychology Clinic, both of which are in Madison, Wisconsin.

I have a Recovery Coaching business which works with families or individuals seeking an alternative approach to dealing with addictions. This is not the therapy model most clients expect. Instead, it is a 3-6 month contract where I am available to them 24/7 by phone, computer or in my office. As a recovery coach I use a collaborative approach with my clients. Although this approach seems on the surface to be more informal and collaborative, it is backed up by my 20 years of professional psychotherapy and addiction therapy experience.

The recovery coaching approach doesn't place me in the role of 'expert.' Instead, I rely on my clients for their self knowledge just as they rely on my skills and experience. People struggling with triggers and powerful urges need me every day. While working with them, I may recommend that they go to AA because it works well for millions of people. But I also offer an individualized and very effective follow-up. I feel strongly about this, especially because the follow-up component was always missing in my own attempts at recovery. I might have lunch or coffee with them. I may take them to their AA meetings. Or I may talk to them on the phone or via email to help them get through a bad patch. In this way, they are able to be out in the world, and not in a structured group environment, but they are still connected to someone who is uniquely qualified to help them. I believe that this process allows them to maintain their dignity and a connection to a normal existence.

I started a Mindfulness group for therapists because I saw the need for professionals in a stressful business to support and help one another. In the process, the participants in this group have become good friends as well as professional colleagues. I love my work, but like other therapists, I feel pain when I lose clients because of their inability to stay sober or because they have committed suicide. And I feel great stress and a strong sense of responsibility when I work with young children who have a parent who is suffering with or dying of substance abuse. The work I do is never easy, but in many ways, my grueling personal experience adds a very useful dimension to my ability to help clients. I am constantly motivated by the number of clients I have worked with whose lives—like my own—have been dramatically changed by their hard-won sobriety.

For much of my life, I was trying to fill what felt like a hole in my psyche in order to make myself feel better. The one-night-stands and the relationships with losers mixed with the constant flow of alcohol were temporary fixes. They were my broken attempt to fill up that empty place that existed somewhere in my soul. When I work with women now, I ask them if they feel they are trying to fill a hole somewhere inside themselves. Often they say they do. Some of them say I am the first person they have met who can relate to them and their addiction problems. After all, I have been through what they are going through. I have struggled mightily with addiction and failure. Now I can be perfectly honest about myself. I can help by giving them what I learned the hard way.

Sometimes as a therapist I feel like Wendy talking to the lost boys in *Peter Pan*. Women who struggle with alcoholism seem to feel safe in my sessions when they don't feel safe anywhere else. They trust me. I am non-judgmental and easily laugh at myself and they find that comforting and helpful. It seems that in the field of addiction, people generally prefer to work with someone who has been through what they are going through. My personal story gives me a great deal of 'street cred'. I don't wave my story in their faces, but I understand the power of it and don't hesitate to use it with certain difficult or skeptical patients who are resisting treatment.

The fact is, it is generally very hard for a non-alcoholic to understand how someone simply cannot stop drinking. Addicts do not want to hear a therapist say, "Just stop drinking," although some say just that. It's not helpful. Two of my patients who recently relapsed have said, "I don't know why this happened. Things were going well for me." I know how it is. I remind them that in some people there is physical evidence that the compulsion to continue the addiction is so strong that it overpowers all other feelings and priorities. Alcoholism is a feelings kind of disease. Addicts want to numb their bad feelings and they turn to alcohol to do that. People say to me, "I just want to run away." I know from my own experience that they want to run to a bottle or some other addiction in order to alter the way they feel.

I believe that therapy should get people into the real world, not keep them in a sequestered cult-like situation they are afraid to leave for fear of relapsing. Everyone is different, but strategies that exist outside the structured boundaries of established therapies often work well for certain types of people. My own brand of spirituality has worked well for me. I don't go to AA every day. But I do pray every day and often get my needs met by a solitary walk in the woods with my dog. I feel a deep spiritual connection when I am alone in a woodsy setting and that sensation helps keep me balanced.

These days, I am no longer praying for my own sobriety. Instead, I am praying to God and saying how grateful I am for where I am today. I am grateful for my children, my husband, my grandchildren, my practice, my dog. Sometimes I pray before I see a patient. I ask that I will have the right words for that patient. Sometimes the right words just flow out of me when I am working with a patient, and I thank God for that even while it is happening.

I am often asked by well-meaning people, "What is the best way to get and stay sober?" They are understandably curious when they learn that I was a patient in over thirty treatment facilities. I am not one who thinks there is only one treatment that works for all people. Alcoholism is a very complex disease that brings with it many underlying mental health issues as well as the old nature vs. nurture debate. The history of addiction treatment has historically been based upon the 12 steps of Alcoholics Anonymous which was founded by Bill Wilson. Many of our country's well-recognized treatment facilities—like Hazelden, where I was both a patient and a therapist—are based on the Minnesota Model in which the 12 steps are a strong component of recovery programs. This is also true of most of the treatment facilities throughout the United States.

I have been sober for over 20 years now and have been work-ing in the field of addiction for much of that time. In my work, I have been exploring alternative methods that might appeal to those clients who dislike AA or have continued to relapse after attending many outpatient or inpatient treatment centers. I rec-ognize that every client I work with has a uniquely personal set of issues—mental, physical or spiritual. I collaborate with them to find what might be the best approach to becoming sober, and also to keep them going in recovery. It is not an easy task and is often filled with disappointment and many setbacks before suc-cess is reached.

In my own case, I know I was afraid of getting sober or show-ing some measure of success. Time and time again I sabotaged a month or two of sober time by picking up a drink again and be-coming that person I could best relate to—the fucked-up drunk. I had no idea how I could be a success, ever. Even today I have days of extreme self doubt and wonder, *Am I for real this time?* When I begin to feel sadness about the way I left my young children, I am appalled. It feels as if I am watching a video of a complete stranger who only looks like me. But I know that when the sad-ness creeps in, I will no longer be tempted to escape with alcohol. Instead, I let the tears flow while sitting at my desk or while driv-ing my car. Oddly, these tears feel good; they show me that I have feelings again! To feel again is one of the benefits of being sober. Feelings and emotions allow me to reclaim my humanity.

Life for me today can still be a roller coaster of personal emo-tions. But now I have a profound faith and I have begun to like myself better, warts and all. The spirit inside me—once controlled by the all-consuming spirit of alcohol—is now a gentle and lov-ing spirit. I can access this spirit through meditation, social sup-port, hiking in the woods, and the feeling of extreme gratitude that I now have my five children back in my life. I have learned to be responsible for my own happiness and my own feelings of self worth.

I believe that all my clients are capable of the changes I have achieved. But they have to want them enough. There is no treat-ment facility, therapist, or 12-step group that can give it to them if they don't feel the need to change. It comes from within. In my work I try to touch that singular light in each client that signals the willingness to make a change despite the strong fear of moving out of the false comfort zone created by addiction. Each journey is different and I am only one sober woman trying to make a difference in another person's future.

In their willingness to allow me to re-enter their lives, my children have gone far beyond all of my most hopeful expectations. I know that each of them has been deeply and painfully affected by the person I was and the role that alcohol played in my ability to be their mother. I am exceedingly grateful that they are successful adults and loving parents in spite of the trauma I caused them. Today they all struggle with various issues in their relationships that can be directly traced back to me. Some of them are commitment-phobic. Others say they have trouble trusting another person. Some of them have struggled with the "frozen tears syndrome" in which you are not crying all the time, but you are kind of frozen with sadness. One of my girls ended up in a psychiatric hospital as a teenager because she was depressed and experienced suicidal thoughts when she had trouble getting along with her stepmother. It hurts me to recognize that I have caused my children ongoing problems, but I am continually delighted by their resilience and generosity of spirit. But they should have their own last words on the subject.

Hallie: I have forgiven my mother because she got well. I feel that she has worked hard to build a relationship and be a mother for us, despite all the years she couldn't be. My siblings and I don't want to hurt her now, so we don't tell her all the stories we have about those bad years. I think it's hard for her to really sit still and hear those stories. We understand it can be very painful. However, when she was helping me with Colby as a newborn, I brought up some of the pain she had caused. I don't remember her ever saying she was sorry, but she broke down crying and fell apart. I don't really want to go there because ours is a beautiful relationship now.

I feel particularly strong because of everything I have overcome in my life and because I am grateful for many things despite a lot of crud that happened. But I will say that Mommy's behavior made me consciously decide to become the opposite of my mother. I took great care to become the mother I had fantasized about as a child.

Lindsey: I didn't just give my mother my forgiveness; she had to earn it. My number one criterion was that she remain sober. Once sober, she had to be honest with herself and with us. My father always stressed, "You only have one biological mother," and she is mine. In finding forgiveness, I was able find happiness and move forward in life. She was not impervious to life's struggles, no one is. But family is the root of everything, good and bad. It can be the root for someone's addiction, and simultaneously can be the source for someone's sobriety. Extending forgiveness to my mother meant I had the benefit of her in my life forever. She was doing her work, and it was time for me to do mine.

Courtney: To my utter amazement—and defying all odds against her—my mother did one day get sober. This time is was for real! Nevertheless, for many years we were still on edge and waiting for her to slip up again and return to the life she lived for so long, on the death road. BUT, this did not happen. Something magical happened to her around the time her mother passed away. Finally, my mother got the strength and will to live—not only to just live but to get herself a real life. She went back to school and got a Master's degree. She became a support to others—a counselor, a mentor, a life savior to others in a position similar to hers in that drinking life she had.

People wonder what my relationship has become with my mother. After years of letdowns and abandonment, did I find forgiveness to let her into my life again? I personally believe holding onto anger or resentment takes up too much of one's soul. So I let those feelings go. I knew that I wanted my mom back in my life, and in order for that to happen, I had to look forward. The truth is, I never had to look far into my heart to forgive her. What did take time was getting to trust her fully again and believing that she was here to stay and choosing the road of life instead of the road of death. I had to learn to believe that she was here to be a mom for me, not just a visitor in and out of my life, but a stable person who I could trust and love. She accepts my love and appreciates it and I can see that her life is now better because of it. She is my mom and I now enjoy every minute I get to spend with her. I look forward to when she calls each week just to say hello and let me know she's thinking of me. My heart and life now feels whole because my mom is in it, and I know she isn't going anywhere.

Today Jane is one of the most respected professionals in her field, because she lived to tell her story and because of what she overcame. She is effective because she has experienced so much of what her clients have and knows how to reach them. She has what is called 'adaptive expertise' and she can feel her clients' pain and sympathize with their struggles. She knows how to reach her clients in a way that many other counselors cannot. She can reach into her memory and pull out what they need. She knows how alcoholism can tear a family apart, and now she knows from experience that you can overcome it.

Tyler: If it wasn't for Courtney insisting that I join her for visits to see my mom in Farmington, I would have seen my mother even less in those years. My lack of desire to see my mom was in part related to my lack of desire to spend time with her, but it was also because I wanted her to feel pain in my absence. I never really held any cards of influence or power and in hindsight there should have been more enforced separation. I know that my dad was very supportive of my mom, and didn't want to restrict access to the kids, or our access to her, but I know that from my perspective there were some very hard years of trying to share a life with my mom. It was difficult for me to go from hitting a nadir of wishing my mom dead, to then have to endure subsequent years of contrived get togethers.

Because of my experience, I have a heightened awareness and sensitivity to alcohol and drinking. Alcoholism is something that I always associated with my two grandfathers, my mom, stepmother, uncles, and to a certain extent, my father. However, I was fortunate to develop an understanding and respect for alcohol. I recall my father making the distinction between functional alcoholism and my mom's. Essentially he made it clear that people have very different relationships with alcohol. He was somehow in another category – one of consistent social abuse. As a result, he was a self-proclaimed "realist" who knew that kids were going to experiment with alcohol and was somewhat of a nurturing figure in that regard. He always instilled in us, and me in particular, that it was okay to drink but that you had to work for it – exercise, not sleep in hung-over, get up and work. My friends were always conflicted about taking advantage of my father's hospitality because they might be able to drink at our house, but then they'd have to wake up early and rake, mow, etc. But I suppose that I've always been somewhat suspicious about women who I see abusing hard alcohol, vodka in particular. It's certainly not the fairest judgment to lay on people, but I suppose we all have our biases.

My husband Don has never seen me drinking or drunk; my past is not something we talk about, although he is very much aware that I came to him with a dark alcoholic history. But even without a clear view of the person I was, he has always been aware that since we have been together, I have become the person I was meant to be.

Don: Jane has been in Madison and married to me for almost ten years, which is half her sober life. Ten years is a long time. She has changed a lot in those years. The longest she was married to any previous husband was seven years.

It's from Madison that she found the confidence to be able to study hard to pass the exam for a license in Marriage and Family Therapy. Concentrating is hard for her, and the exam, written by the certified professionals in her field, is reputedly one of the hardest for a therapist to pass. After several tries, she passed and became a licensed pro in Madison. In her field, anyone can hang out a shingle, but sensible clients, like insurance companies, will only pay for therapy from a licensed professional.

It's from Madison that she re-connected with her family. Both through group reunion visits and through one-on-one visits, her children got to know her again. She is now a trusted and well-loved parent. They ask her for advice on difficult issues, whereas before they did not.

In Madison, she has learned about herself. She now knows how nature can restore her. She can temporarily put aside her cares and responsibilities to sit or walk in the woods. She can say in mid-week, "I'm going to the woods tomorrow," when she needs a boost.

In Madison, she has developed her once-dormant love of many things such as classical music. She now knows that the music she likes best is that of the Eastern Europeans and Russians of 100 years ago. She keeps CDs by Dvorak and Rachmaninoff in her car.

Jane retains her wild side and has many speeding tickets. When the plowed driveway has an inch of packed snow on it, she rockets down it on a sled, occasionally crashing into a hard snow bank. She walks on the ice on our creek, despite the occasional warning that the ice is too thin. Once she fell through into freezing water up to her waist. This led to a fast half-mile walk to our cabin while her clothes were freezing to her. She has walked on ice on the Wisconsin River. Slipping into a hole there is known to be a sure death. The fast moving current under the ice will suck you under and down river. To where? We say to New Orleans, where the Chinese chefs make you into a wonderful Jambalaya.

So it's in Madison that she finally flowered into a confident woman and professional. We've been in groups at parties where she is the only person without a PhD, yet she is the one who gets pumped for information and is respected for her expertise. The contrast to her previous life is enormous. What a waste it would be for her to be a drunk. Jane has said to me, "In Madison, I became the real me."

Sadly, my brother Bruce died of cancer in the fall of 2011. As I sat in a pew listening to the moving service in his honor and the readings from his sons, I grabbed onto my brother Tom's hand and he lovingly handed me his handkerchief. As we hung onto one another and sang *Amazing Grace*, I felt a surge of love for Tom. This feeling had for a very long time been dulled by the confusing memory of that long ago encounter in his bedroom.

As I stood next to Tom in that moment, I thought about the blessed forgiveness granted to me by my children for the misery and grief I caused them and realized that this was the time for me to let go of any remaining feelings of self pity and denial and forgive my brother and everyone else I had blamed for things that inexplicably happened many years ago. I have long understood that no one act and no one person drove me to alcoholism. I know I was already in the gene pool for alcohol addiction and I also know that my own confused need to seek love and approval created a toxic mix and helped propel me into addiction.

What I thought of as my 'lost' childhood self is now connected to a much stronger, more grateful self and the only important thing to understand is that through my own efforts and through an abundance of grace, I have managed to prevail with the best part of me intact. My life is now useful and good. For that I am truly grateful.

L-R, Hallie, Kris, Courtney, Jane, Tyler, Lindsey.

Acknowledgements

You never know how things are going to come together. I met my ghostwriter Tansy Blumer several years ago. While talking to her, my recovery story tumbled out of me, and at the end of it she handed me her business card and offered to help me write a book. A year later I was at an addiction counseling conference in Washington, DC and invited her to dinner. The rest, as they say, is history. I would not have been able to write this book without Tansy. She directed me, encouraged me, kicked my ass on several occasions, and handed me tissues when difficult memories got to my heart. She also encouraged my five children to participate fully in the project and interviewed my ex-husband, Ron, at the house we bought together and where my children grew up.

My oldest daughter Kris added an honest and moving voice to my story; as always, she spoke from her heart. My other children also dug deep; it took courage for them to remember things they would like to forget.

Ron Ronald has been an inspiration to all who know him. He had to raise five children when I left. The credit for keeping them psychologically whole goes to him and the love he received from his own mother, Evelyn Ronald, who died recently at the age of 101. She never gave up on me, even at my worst.

Don Nichols, my husband of 11 years, has never once looked at me differently or loved me less because of my alcoholism. He has constantly encouraged me to write this story of hope because he felt it would help me finally have some closure and forgive myself. He was right.

I am also grateful to the hundreds of clients I have worked with over the past 20 years. I suspect I have learned more from them than they have learned from me. They have inspired me with their own stories and have left me with a deeper sense of gratitude for my own recovery. Their struggles remind me over and over of what I could have lost forever.

The Authors

Jane Bartels is presently in private practice in Madison, Wisconsin as a psychotherapist, specializing in families affected by substance abuse. She runs groups for women, men, adolescents, and children ages 7 – 12, and she provides individual therapy for mental health issues. Bartels is a clinical member of the American Association of Marriage and Family Therapists (AAMFT), has been a Certified Addictions Counselor since 1990, and is a CSAC in the State of Wisconsin.

The heart of Ms. Bartels' Recovery Coaching Practice, called *Recovery Through Balance*, is an approach which stands on the cutting edge of therapy because it combines therapy and coaching to help clients immediately after their release from recovery programs as well as those who cannot afford to go to professional recovery programs.

Ms. Bartels has personally undergone over thirty treatments and hospitalizations due to her alcohol addiction and is now in total recovery and has established her "street cred" with a succession of patients who were reluctant to work with therapists who have not "been there" as addicts themselves. She earned a BS in Psychology at the age of 50 from Smith College in Northampton, Massachusetts where she was an Ada Comstock Scholar. She earned a M.Ed. in Clinical Psychology at Springfield College in Springfield. Having "crossed over" from addict to counselor, Ms. Bartels has been a successful practitioner in several of the programs in which she was formerly a patient. Among these are Hazelden, in Chicago, Illinois, and the Institute of Living in Hartford, Connecticut. She has also been a consultant to the State of Connecticut in its efforts to set up and run the Fresh Start program, a supervised halfway house alternative to prison for women with children.

Tansy Howard Blumer lives in Washington, D.C. with her husband and has two grown daughters. She is a graduate of Smith College and has an MA degree from the University of Maryland Graduate School. Tansy's love of journalistic, non-fiction writing led her to change her career course in 2002 to ghostwrite memoirs—both private and commercial. She has written 8 memoirs for private clients. To date, two commercially published memoirs are:

- *Big Man on Campus – A University President Speaks Out on Higher Education* by Stephen Joel Trachtenberg with Tansy Howard Blumer, Touchstone, Simon & Schuster, NYC (2008) (hardcover and paperback) and;
- *What's the Beef? Sixty Years of Hard-Won Lessons for Today's Leaders in Labor, Management and Government*, by Wayne L. Horvitz with Tansy Howard Blumer, Hamilton Books, Lanham, MD (2009) (paperback);